Books by Janice Hardy

Foundations of Fiction
Plotting Your Novel: Ideas and Structure
Plotting Your Novel Workbook
Revising Your Novel: First Draft to Finished Draft Series
Book One: Fixing Your Character & Point-of-View Problems
Book Two: Fixing Your Plot & Story Structure Problems
Book Three: Fixing Your Setting & Description Problems

Skill Builders
Understanding Show, Don't Tell (And Really *Getting It)*
Understanding Conflict (And What It Really *Means)*

Novels
The Healing Wars Trilogy:
The Shifter
Blue Fire
Darkfall

As J.T. Hardy
Blood Ties

Published by Janice Hardy
Printed in the United States of America.

This book is also available in e-book format.

ISBN 978-1-948305-93-8

Fixing Your Plot & Story Structure Problems

Book Two of Revising Your Novel:
First Draft to Finished Draft

Janice Hardy

Fiction University's Foundations of Fiction

Contents

49   Workshop Two: Plot and Structure Work

Welcome to Book Two of Revising Your Novel: *Fixing Your Plot and Story Structure Problems*

There's something both exhilarating and terrifying about finishing a first draft. The story is finally written down, and you've seen how your characters have grown and developed, but you also see all the plot holes, weak areas, and parts you know for sure don't work.

Most of the time, turning that first draft into the novel in your head takes work. A lot of work.

My goal with this series is to help writers of all skill levels revise a first draft, and help you develop your rough manuscript into a finished draft. This series will provide guidance if you're new to revisions, and work as a stand-in critique partner if you're not yet ready to show the manuscript to another person. It will help you determine which revision techniques and processes work best for you, how to think about the revision process, and how to put those skills into practice.

To help make the process more manageable, I've broken the original *Revising Your Novel: First Draft to Finished Draft* into three smaller books. Book One is *Fixing Your Character and Point-of-View Problems*, focusing on character-specific aspects such as, characters, point of view, dialogue, internalization, and theme. Book Two is *Fixing Your Plot and Story Structure Problems*, taking a closer look at plotting, scene and story structure, and pacing. Book Three is *Fixing Your Setting and Description*

Problems, digging into setting, world building, and description. At times, a problem in one area could be due to issues in another area, such as a character motivation issue that's really a plot problem, and I'll refer you to another book in those cases. There is also an omnibus version containing all three books for those who prefer one guide.

Please note that some aspects of revision carry over regardless of what you're revising, so there will be some duplication within the three books in the series—such as preparing to revise and getting ready for revising your manuscript (as well as this welcome letter). The prep work sessions and Workshop One are roughly the same in each book, as are the final workshops that look at word count and the entire manuscript—which might reveal issues in other areas you didn't realize you had.

Just as there is no right way to write, there's no right way to revise. It's a process every writer must work out for themselves, and can even vary from book to book. You never know what extra effort a manuscript will need until you see how that first draft shakes out.

For first-time revisers, this can be overwhelming. There's so much to consider, keep track of, and remember. They often don't know how to start or what to work on first.

For seasoned writers, it can be just as intimidating, especially if revision isn't something they enjoy doing.

For those of us who love revisions and do our best writing after we know how the story unfolds, it's still a lot of work. Fun work, but there's still a long way to go from "the end" to "It's done!"

But I'm here to help with that.

Ready to go? Then roll up your sleeves and let's get to work

What You'll Get From This Book

Fixing Your Plot and Story Structure Problems is a mix of book doctor and personal editor. The goal of the analysis sections is to help you develop your book doctor skills and teach you what you need to objectively review your manuscript. The revision steps and options will guide you to the best way to fix any issues you'll find during your analysis.

You'll review the manuscript from the top down, looking at the larger macro issues of structure and plot, all the way to the micro issues of how an individual scene works. You'll focus on the pieces and how they fit within the larger framework of the novel.

There's a *lot* of information in these pages. Take it session by session and work at a pace that's comfortable for you. No one expects you to revise an entire novel over a weekend, so don't worry if it takes you more time. Revising a novel is often hard work, but well worth it in the end.

This information is here to guide you, encourage you, give you goals to strive for, and most of all—help you.

By the end of the workshops, you'll have a clean, well-developed plot that's ready to move on to the next step.

Whatever your goal for your novel, this book will help you get there.

What You'll Encounter in This Book

Fixing Your Plot and Story Structure Problems is a series of self-guided workshops designed to lead writers through the revision process. Each workshop covers one step of that process, with smaller sessions that focus on individual topics within that step. At the end of this book, you'll have a cleaner manuscript and a novel that fits your vision.

Workshops: The workshops go step by step through revising a novel. Each workshop offers topics with questions, directions, tips and tricks, plus common problem areas within each topic and suggestions on how to fix them.

Analysis: Each workshop starts with an analysis that examines an aspect of the manuscript and helps you determine where any weak spots might be.

Revision Tasks: These go step by step with tasks to do, or further questions to ask to fix the problems found in the analysis.

Revision Options: Most workshops offer multiple options on how to revise that aspect of the manuscript, focusing on the most common problems in that area.

Revision Red Flags: These prompts draw attention to common problems found in early drafts of a novel.

Problems Found? These prompts suggest where to go to solve problems found during the workshop analysis.

How to Get the Most From the Sessions

I've structured *Fixing Your Plot and Story Structure Problems* in a way I find the most helpful when revising, but feel free to adjust the order of the workshops to best suit your own writing process.

If you know what plot and structure areas you want to work on already, feel free to jump ahead to the workshops that fit your needs. Use this book to guide you, but don't feel you must follow every last suggestion and do every single option. This is why I'll frequently say, "probably" "likely," and "often" throughout this book, and suggest things to "try," "consider," and "think about." Just because advice or a technique typically works a certain way, every novel *is* different and what you're trying to achieve with it must be taken into consideration when applying my advice and tips.

Different manuscripts have different issues, so focus on what *your* novel needs. If something suggested here doesn't apply, it's okay to ignore it; just be objective and honest about what the manuscript needs. If you feel you're strong in an area and skip a section, but still can't fix a particular problem, try looking at those sections anyway. You might find the answer you need is there after all, for example, writers with strong goal−>conflict−>resolution skills might over plot and run into pacing problems.

Revising a novel is just as much about studying the story as it is tweaking the text, and the analysis sessions were designed to help you examine your manuscript objectively. Some questions will be easy to answer, focusing on general reminders and clarification aspects of the novel, while others will be tougher and require hard looks at the manuscript. There will likely be times when answering these questions feels too hard or not necessary, but this is where the real work lies—it's difficult to revise a novel when you don't know where it's weak.

The more effort you put into figuring out what your manuscript needs, the better prepared you'll be to meet those needs.

Getting Ready to Revise

Sometimes, you *think* you're ready to revise, but there's often a period between finishing a first draft and starting the first revision when you're "done" with the manuscript, even though you still have a few tasks left to do. You're tired of drafting; you want to move on to revising and get the novel out the door.

This can be a dangerous time, because if you jump in before the manuscript is truly finished, you'll create more work for yourself. The rougher that first draft is, the more prep work you might need to do. However, if you tend to write clean first drafts, you might indeed be ready to move forward and start your revisions.

Be objective and honest. The more truthful you are regarding the state of your draft, the better prepared you'll be to revise it.

Take a little time and finish a not-quite-done-yet-draft (if needed), run it through your beta readers, get organized, and mentally prepare for all the work you're about to do.

First, Fill the Holes

Look at your manuscript objectively—is it *really* ready or do you still have a few holes to fill? (Be honest.) It's not unusual to have a manuscript with a few holes that you promise you'll "fix in revision." Sometimes you *can* fix these holes while you revise, but other times they need filling before you move forward.

In this session, the goal is to finish the first draft before you begin your revision.

Step One: Finish (or Write) Any Scenes You've Been Putting Off

There are always one or two scenes you know you *need* to write, but never *do* write until you absolutely have to. If you have any scenes you've been putting off, sit your butt in the chair and write them. Even if they're clunky and messy, at least they'll be down on paper where you can fix them. And if they fight you, maybe that's a red flag you don't need them after all (wouldn't *that* be a relief?).

Step Two: Fill in the Details That Still Require Research

Look for places where knowing a detail wasn't necessary during the first draft, but adding it now *will* make the scene richer and more plausible.

Pick a day when you can focus, then start at the first missing detail and take them one at a time until they're done. At the very least, write the information in another file so you can easily add it when you reach that scene during revision.

Step Three: Finalize Any Shaky Character Backstories

Odds are the main characters have decent backstories and histories (if not, you can deal with that in *Book Two: Fixing Your Character and Point-of-View Problems*), but secondary characters—or characters who turned out to be more important than you originally thought—might not be as fleshed out as needed.

Look at your characters and flesh out any missing histories or defining moments necessary to the plot. Now that the first draft is done, it should be clear who matters and who needs more oomph to refine their personalities or personal stories. You'll also know what areas or details will add depth to the existing story and character arcs.

Step Four: Decide on the Final Details or Names

Sometimes you need to live with a name or detail a while before you decide if they're working in the novel or not. And sometimes, you change them mid-novel and forget, so both versions (or spellings) exist.

If you have any names or details you're not sure about, change them now so you can get used to the new ones, and change them again if you still don't like them.

Step Five: Do What You Know Needs Doing

If there's anything you think is going to take additional time or effort, go ahead and do some work on it first. Maybe you know you're not happy about the setting, or you wanted to add more symbolism, or you think the novel needs a subplot—whatever is nagging at you, give in and fix it. Filling the holes now will make the rest of the revision process easier.

Optional: Hand the Manuscript Off to Beta Readers or Critique Partners

Not every writer seeks feedback at the same stage (if at all). If you prefer to receive feedback before you do your revision, send your draft to your critique partners when the draft is done. If you'd rather get the manuscript as finished as possible before looking for feedback, then do your revision first. When (and if) you seek feedback is totally up to you.

Know When to Revise What

Unless you're one of those rare authors who can write and polish a novel in one draft, you'll go through several revision passes between the first and finished drafts. How many passes depends on both the novel and the writer, and you might do as few as two or as many as twenty. No matter how many drafts a novel needs, you *can* make the process more efficient. For example, it doesn't make much sense to polish the text if you're still figuring out the story.

In this session, the goal is to understand the most effective way to do your revision so you're not revising text you've already edited.

Early Draft Revisions

These revisions take the most rewriting, so tackle them first. They change how the plot and story unfold, who the characters are, maybe even the theme, but don't typically affect how the text itself reads (unless you decide to change narrative styles, such as past tense to present tense or first person to third). In early draft revisions you will:

Get the story the way you want it: This is the story you wanted to tell, even if it still needs some work. It illustrates your idea and conveys the concepts you wanted to explore. If the story isn't working, the most beautifully written prose in the world won't save it.

Get the plot the way you want it: Everyone in the story has the right goals and is generally doing what they need to do. Revising your plot is all about moving the pieces around so they're in the best possible places to achieve the strongest impact. For example, you might know you need a scene where the protagonist discovers her best friend betrayed her, but not know exactly where that scene best fits in the novel.

Get the characters the way you want them: Characters change over the course of a novel, and not just in the story. You might start a character with one personality and end up changing it as the novel develops. Or you might decide two minor characters should be combined into one, or kill off a character altogether. Make sure you have the right story people in the right places.

Middle Draft Revisions

Once you've dealt with the macro issues, move on to the text itself. Middle draft revisions include issues that require rewriting on a smaller, scene-by-scene level. These edits don't change the plot or story, but clarify or enhance how the information is conveyed to your readers. In middle draft revisions you will:

Flesh out or cut descriptions: Descriptions almost always need revising. You'll trim heavy areas and bulk up sparse ones, fix talking heads in empty rooms, and generally ground readers in every scene. You'll cut descriptive elements that aren't working to dramatize and/or set the scene.

Adjust the pacing and scene or chapter transitions: A novel's flow determines how readers experience the story. Awkward transitions and episodic chapters can kill the pacing instead of building tension and drawing readers in. You'll tighten the overall novel and cut out any dead weight dragging it down.

Replace weak words and phrases with strong ones: Some word edits require more rewriting than others, and this is a good revision pass to take right before the final polish pass. You'll tweak the text and make sure everything reads well.

Finished Draft Revisions

The final revision pass is all about the last-minute review, fixing the elements that have been nagging at you, or clearing up any messy areas. Most scenes require little more than a cut here and there or moving a sentence for better narrative flow. In finished draft revisions you will:

Tweak little aspects: Minor tweaks, such as moving a comma or changing a word, gets smoothed over.

Drive yourself crazy deciding if it's done or not: We all do it. The manuscript seems finished, but self-doubt nags you and you start second-guessing every decision you made. If it's only general fears, you're ready to go. If they're specific, your writer's instinct is likely trying to tell you there's still a problem to address. Go examine it further and either fix it, or put those doubts to rest.

Read the manuscript one last time: A final read is useful for catching leftover edits or details that no longer apply. It's also good to check the final flow of the story and how it all unfolds. This pass is particularly useful after letting the manuscript sit for a few weeks so you can read it with fresh eyes and see what's actually on the page. You'll make one last pass before you stop messing with the story and turn to the copyedits.

Final Draft Polish

Once the manuscript is working and everything reads smoothly, it's time for the final polish to put the shine on the prose. These edits that don't change the story, plot, or understanding of either, just how the text itself reads. The goal in this final pass is to focus on the copy editing and proofing.

Check for oft-used or repeated words: We all have favorite words or phrases and we tend to use them a lot. You'll read through and trim out anything that sounds repetitious.

Catch any revision smudge: In any revision, you'll find leftover bits that refer or relate to something you edited out. Details change, time of day moves from morning to night, characters refer to something (or someone) that was later deleted. A final read through in one sitting can help make those smudges jump out, especially if you haven't looked at the manuscript in a few weeks.

Check the spelling, punctuation, and grammar: Break out those dictionaries and style rules to catch any technical errors, dropped punctuation, incorrect word usage, and typos—especially those sneaky little homonyms such as their, there, and they're. If you're unsure of a rule or word, look it up.

Check any spellings or details unique to your novel: If you've created names or items, it's not a bad idea to check to ensure every instance is spelled the same way and used consistently. This is a must if you changed the name of anything midway through writing the draft. Odds are you missed one somewhere.

Working from the macro to the micro issues can make the revision process go more smoothly, regardless of how many drafts you do. It also gives you a structure that makes revising a little less intimidating. You know what to worry about when, and you can ignore elements that don't need your attention in that revision pass.

Mentally Prepare Yourself for the Revision

Not every writer dreads a revision, but if the thought of revising is daunting or even frightening, it helps to mentally prepare for the work involved, especially if you know you have a lot of rewriting to do. By the time a novel is written, the characters feel like family, and anything you do to alter that family *can* be rough. Even if you enjoy revising, it's helpful to prepare for it.

In this session, the goal is to put yourself in the right mindset to have productive and effective revision sessions.

Don't Be Afraid of the Delete Key

I learned long ago that trying to force in a favorite line or scene makes that line or scene *sound* forced and it ends up not working anyway. Remember, your words aren't set in stone. You're the writer, you *can* change the text however you want, and that's okay because you're still *writing*. Delete chapters without a thought if they need to go; cut favorite lines if the scene changes and they no longer work. It's still a work in progress until you decide it's done.

It's the Story That Matters

Focusing on the story makes it easier to accept any big changes you might need to do. Plots change all the time, but the heart of the story usually stays the same. Don't be afraid to re-plot or make drastic changes if it will make the story better. The plot is only a series of events that illustrate the story, and you have tons of options for getting to the same place.

REVISION RED FLAG: If you find yourself changing the *story* as well as the plot, you might have a core conflict issue or story premise problem. It only becomes problematic if you're changing the plot and story so much, every revision reads like a whole new book. You're basically trying to write and revise the draft at the same time, which is bound to cause frustration. Nail down the story you want to tell first, *then* go back and create the plot to show that story.

First Drafts Are for Ideas

A first draft doesn't need to be perfect, or even be the book you expected. Stories evolve, plots change, so feel free to move around major plot events to see how they play out. Decide what you want to do, and if you like the new direction, proceed to revise. If it's not what you want, keep drafting until it is. No one says you have to revise the *first* first draft.

Making the Story Better is a Good Idea, Even if it Takes Work

"But that'll be so much work" is a common reason not to make a change, but it's a bad one. You've already put a ton of work into the book, so why not make it the best it can be and give it the best chance to sell? Embrace the work, because "writing" isn't only done during the first draft. Some of the best writing can come *after* several drafts when you can see how all the pieces work together.

REVISION RED FLAG: If you find yourself adding more and more extraneous plot points or story arcs to the novel to "make it better" and very little of it affects the core conflict of the novel, you probably have too much going on. Don't add more to add more—make sure what you add is serving the story you're telling.

Think Macro Until You're Happy With the Story

The big elements determine if a novel will work—the core conflicts, the character goals, the stakes, the premise. If these aren't working, no matter how much you polish the scenes or the writing, the story will feel *bleh*. Major inherent story flaws need to be fixed before the book as a whole can work.

Trust Your Gut

If you think something needs fixing, it probably does. If it nags at you that a certain character does a certain thing, go fix it before you put a ton of work into revising. If that big reveal doesn't have the impact you think it should, change it. If anything bugs you, trust your writer's compass and work it out until you're happy.

Revising taps into a slightly different part of the writer's brain, so the better you mentally prepare, the easier your revisions will be.

Stay Organized During the Revision

How much feedback the manuscript gets before you start revising will determine how much you have to keep track of. Detailed critiques from your ten best beta readers will yield a lot more information than looking at the first draft with no outside comments. How many changes you plan to do also plays a role, as well as the state of the manuscript at the start. Keeping track of it all *can* be challenging.

In this session, the goal is to determine the best way to organize your thoughts and keep track of what you want to do.

Step One: Gather Your Materials

Some writers like index cards and tape flags, others use three-ring binders and highlighters, and still others use software with electronic files instead of manila folders. Whatever your preferred manner, get everything you'll use so you'll have it handy when you need it. Don't forget about the non-writing essentials—your favorite drink or snack, reference guides, links to blog posts with helpful advice (such as Fiction University). If you think you'll need it, put it within reach.

If you don't have a preferred method yet (or don't think your current one is working), try one or more of these options:

Software: Collect all your notes and critiques in one file (or folder) in your favorite program. Microsoft Word's Document Map feature is a handy way to create a table of contents to quickly scan through for what you want. Scrivener allows you to add text sub-files with everything you need right there per scene or chapter. Note-taking software, such as Microsoft's OneNote or Evernote, is another way to keep everything in one place.

Three-ring binders and paper: For those who prefer a more hands-on approach, a binder with paper you can add to and group how you like it can be the perfect fit. You can easily add pages, move pages as needed, and take notes anywhere. You might even have a separate binder for the manuscript itself, with notes and ideas written on the pages.

Tape flags and printed pages: If the idea of everything written and marked on the manuscript appeals to you, print out your manuscript and use different colored tape flags for different aspects of the revision. Tape additional sheets of paper to pages for extra notes, or write on the backs of the pages. Don't forget scissors and tape if you go this route. Highlighters and colored pens are also useful.

Step Two: Gather Your Notes

Hunting through files or pages to find the feedback comment you want to address can be both time consuming and annoying. Collect everything in one place so you can easily access it when you reach that section of the revision. Create a story bible with important details to maintain consistency.

If you don't have a preferred method yet (or don't think your current one is working), try any of these options:

Put the notes into the manuscript file: Copy all the comments you want to address directly into the manuscript, so as you read through each scene, you'll see what needs to be done. Macro comments might be added at the start of each chapter or scene, or in the beginning of the file. If you have multiple critiquers, you might use a different color per person. Or you might use a different color per type of problem to address, such as green for point-of-view issues and red for places where you're telling and not showing.

Create a master revision file: A master file with a summary and list of what you want to revise can provide a nice, step-by-step guide to follow—and a checklist to cross off when each aspect is done.

Print everything out: Hard copies you can physically flip through could be a better option for those who prefer to edit from paper.

Use index cards: A popular organization method is to write out what needs to be done per scene on a index card, referencing page numbers or chapters. You can put everything on one card, or use a different color for each character or option.

EXTRA TIP: *Decide how you'll identify what comments have been dealt with. Delete them? Move them to another file or folder? Change the color, or simply cross them off a list? It'll help when you're not sure if you've made a change or not.*

Step Three: Gather Your Thoughts

There's a reason the previous session in this book is called Mentally Prepare Yourself for the Revision. Revising a novel is a lot of work, and being in the wrong head space can affect how productive it is. It's not uncommon to try to tackle too much too fast, and end up frustrated and feeling as though you're not getting anywhere (or worse—that you're ruining the manuscript). Take the time you need to be in the right frame of mind to revise your novel, review your plan, and have fun with it.

Let my advice, tips, and questions help you focus, stay on track, and guide you through your revision so you don't have to worry about what you're forgetting.

Types of Revisions

Not all revisions are created equal. You'll write clean first drafts that fall out of your head onto the page as if they *want* to be written, and drafts that fight you every step of the way until you whip them into submission and make the novel work. Other drafts you'll write and revise countless times until they become a tangled mess (even though you still *love* that story and *swear* you'll make it work).

Approaching one of the less common types of manuscripts often requires a different tack than the average draft—and a little more effort to make it work. But the results can be worth it if it turns that mess of a manuscript into the book of your heart.

Different Types of Revisions

Most writers will have a first draft that's ready for revision. These will be split between manuscripts no one but you has seen, and manuscripts that have been through a round of beta readers or critique partners. The more uncommon revision will be a novel you've revised countless times to make work and need extra help to finally get it there.

In this session, the goal is to determine the type of revision you're facing, and determine if you need to take a slightly different approach. Feel free to skip the specific in-depth sections if you're not facing that type of revision.

Revising on Your Own

This is a typical first-draft revision, where no one but you has seen the manuscript. You either want to work out all the bugs before you show it to anyone, or you want to make sure it's as complete as possible before asking for feedback. For a more in-depth discussion on this revision type, see page 19.

Revising From Feedback

This is a draft that's been through critiques and has feedback to help guide you in your revision. It might be a first draft or a later draft. The hard part here is figuring out what feedback to heed and what to ignore. For a more in-depth discussion on this revision type, see page 20.

Revising Overly Revised Manuscripts (The Frankendraft)

The more troublesome manuscripts are those you've revised over and over. You've changed so much you often forget what story you were trying to write in the first place. These revisions require a slightly different approach than a typical revision. Until you decide what you want, you won't know the steps to take to get there. For a more in-depth discussion on this revision type, see page 26.

Revising From Multiple Drafts

If you've been revising for a while, you might have several drafts that explore different directions. This is especially true if you weren't sure how the story might unfold and needed to write a draft or two to figure it out. Problem is, you're now faced with several drafts that all contain scenes and ideas you like, and you have no clue how to merge them all into one draft. For a more in-depth discussion on this revision type, see page 29.

Revising Half-Finished Manuscripts

These manuscripts have stalled, often somewhere in the middle of the novel. They require more effort because they're often inherently flawed—which is why they're giving you so much trouble—and until you fix that flaw you can't get the novel to work. You love the story, but you don't want to scrap the whole thing and start over—though sometimes this is the only way to get this type of novel to work.

Preparing yourself for the revision at hand helps ensure you revise your novel in the most effective and productive way possible.

If you've identified the type of revision you face, move on for a more in-depth discussion, or jump ahead to Workshop One: Revision Prep if you're ready to start now.

Revising on Your Own

You've finished a first draft, seen how the story unfolded, and are ready to move on to draft number two and strengthen the story and/or fix any problems you've found. You know what it needs and want to get the manuscript into decent shape before you send it out to beta readers or even agents and editors.

In this session, the goal is to separate yourself from your work so you can look at it objectively.

One of the toughest aspects of writing is the ability to look at your work without an emotional attachment to it. Since you wrote it, you understand elements that might not be clear to readers, and you often overlook any flaws your instincts say need to be fixed. To get the most from a revision, you have to look at your work as if you didn't write it.

Give Yourself the Freedom to Stink

First drafts don't always stink, but a lot of them do, so don't worry if yours is one of them. It's normal. Pretty much every writer writes a bad first draft at some point, and it doesn't mean the manuscript is a failure. That first-draft brain dump can be messy, and the revision is how you clean up the mess.

If you're revising on your own, you have to rely on your eyes and instincts to spot issues and fix them. This can be hard if you're too emotionally invested in the work, and every little "mistake" can feel like the end of the world.

It's not.

As you go through your manuscript, remember: You're not finding mistakes, you're finding places to improve the manuscript.

Approach it as if You're Doing a Critique for a Friend

It can help to look at your manuscript and pretend it was written by a friend. What advice would you give that friend about this story?

Take it a step further and pretend it's a good friend who wants you to tell it like it is and not hold back. They won't take anything you say personally. Then critique the manuscript to the best of your ability.

Be a good friend and be ruthless. The tougher you are, the better the manuscript will be.

Don't Worry About the Time it Takes to Revise

Unless you're on a deadline, worrying about when you'll get a revision done can be stressful and sap your creativity and energy. You want to get your book done as quickly as possible so you can send it out, but rushing the work never results in the best work, and this can hurt you and your novel in the long run.

It's okay if it takes longer than you expect to make your novel shine. And if you're *not* worrying about it, you often wind up getting done more quickly anyway, because all that energy is going into the revision, not the worrying.

Revising on your own is a useful way to get your novel the way you want it before showing it to others. You're happy with it and aren't being influenced during the drafting process by outside advice.

Revising From Feedback

Writing is a solitary endeavor, and it's common to fall in love with your words. You've spent a lot of time and effort on your book, so sometimes the thought of changing a single word can be disheartening. It's even harder when other people ask for major changes you're not sure the manuscript needs. But revisions are a part of publishing, and you'll have to find the best way to apply any editorial advice received.

In this session, the goal is to look at ways to best use any feedback received to revise your novel.

It's important to remember that *you* are always in control of your work. You *can* say no to changes—whether they come from critique groups, beta readers, agents, or editors. You decide how you want to handle feedback, and you might find that you can find ways to satisfy critiquers *and* do something you never expected with the book.

First Look at a Critique

Everyone has their own process for handling critique feedback and diving into revisions, but when faced with pages of information and comments, sometimes it's hard to know where to start. A good first step is to simply read them with no expectations. Make no judgments here. If anything pops up that seems totally out of left field (and there's always something unexpected), let it slide on by.

Once you've read everything, ask your critiquers any questions you might have. Sometimes you'll need clarification on a point, or someone will say something that resonates with you and you'll want them to elaborate. After that, let the critique sit for a few days.

The sitting is an important aspect. You no doubt have hopes and dreams for your story, so any negative comment can trigger a knee-jerk reaction and the need to justify *why* you did something. "They're missing the point," you cry. (For the record, they usually aren't.) Letting the feedback soak in helps you evaluate it objectively.

Dealing With Feedback From Critique

When you get a critique it can be easy (and tempting) to ignore what you don't like and accept only the comments that praise the manuscript. But you asked or the "critique" part, so treat any feedback with the respect it deserves. It was given to help you discern where any problems lie in your manuscript, and to give you opportunities to make the work even better.

Take every comment seriously: Even if it seems out of left field or flat out wrong, someone thought it based on what you wrote. Ask yourself *why* the critiquer said it and try to see the underlying problem, *then* decide if it's a comment that needs to be addressed or not. Often, comments that come out of left field are your critiquers picking up on a subtle problem, but even they're not sure what that problem is. They know something is wrong, but guessing as to the real cause. A totally wrong comment *can* be missing the point, but it's still valid since it's what the critiquer felt. It's your job to determine what made that critiquer feel that way and then decide if it needs fixing.

If you agree with a comment, make the change: Sometimes you'll agree with something, but don't want to do it. It'll be too much work, it'll cause another problem later, etc. Do it anyway.

If you don't agree with a comment, don't make the change: It's your book; do what you think is best. Even great ideas or suggestions can be wrong for your novel. As long as you understand why the comment was made and have solid reasons for not addressing it, you can ignore it. It's the comments you disagree with but can't say why that can come back to bite you.

If you're not sure about a comment, think about what the critiquer is trying to point out and why: Think about why you're resistant to the comment. Sometimes feedback requires an edit that scares you, asks you to change something you love, or even needs a skill you're not sure you have to fix. Or it might suggest something you hadn't thought about before, but there's something in the comment that resonates with you and you hesitate. It's as if your subconscious knows there's a gem in that comment.

If you trust the critiquer had that issue, but know in your heart the scene or detail is right: Sometimes critiquers spot a problem and know something is off, but the trouble spot isn't where they see it—it's all in the setup, so the resolution isn't coming through correctly. Critiquers see the *symptoms* of the problem, but not the true cause, and your gut is telling you they're wrong, but...still right. If you fix the issue where they mention it, you don't fix the problem and might even create a new one. But if you consider why they feel that way, you can trace those symptoms back to where you went off track.

If it's a grammar or punctuation rule and you're not sure if the comment is right, look it up: People remember rules wrong all the time, especially when things such as commas *can* be a personal preference. Overall, if a punctuation change makes the sentence read better, make it. If not, don't.

If it's a clarity issue, fix it, even if you think it's clear: If a reader was confused, something wasn't clear. Sure, you may have left hints, or even talked about it two chapters earlier, but if your critiquer read those chapters a week apart (like a reader might) and forgot a key bit of information, another reader will likely have the same problem. You might not need to go deep into anything, but a quick word or two as a reminder usually fixes the uncertainty.

Do whatever serves the story best: Even good ideas can be the wrong ideas if they don't fit the story you're trying to tell. Adding or doing something that seems cool just *because* it's cool *can* hurt your novel. It can hijack it, add unneeded subplots, and confuse the core conflict.

Don't Try to Do it All

As tough as revising can be, the hard part is reviewing your critiques and not being sure what to do with all that advice. It's not uncommon to want to do everything everyone says, but listening *too* hard can *cause* problems. Sometimes it's better to hear what they're saying and identify the problem that made them say it in the first place.

For example, you might get comments such as:

> *Nothing's happening in this scene, you should cut it.* (This could indicate a problem with an unclear goal, and simply making that goal more clear would fix it.)

> *I don't understand why this character is doing this.* Maybe explain what they're really after? (This could indicate a problem with motivation, but explaining the specifics too much will give away the secret and kill the tension.)

> *I don't believe he'd do that here.* (This could indicate a failure to lay the right groundwork leading up to that choice, not a problem with the character's actions.)

It's helpful to consider the source when reviewing your feedback. A mystery fan might nudge you to create more mystery or drop more clues, which might not be appropriate for your romantic comedy. The romance fan might encourage you to develop the sexual tension between the leads, even though there's no romance in the novel. A thriller fan might ask you to pick up the pace, even though a historical fiction fan might prefer a slower pace.

It's possible you're getting such comments because:

- The mystery reader doesn't care about characters and only wants a twisty puzzle to solve (and your novel is a character-driven story).
- The romance reader wants to see the two leads fall in love (and your novel is an adventure story with no romance).
- The thriller reader wants an adrenaline rush with high stakes (and your novel is more suspense with personal stakes).

These readers want what the book is not, and their comments would only push you to write a different type of book than what you intended.

However...it's *possible* you're getting such comments because:

- The mystery reader feels the plot is too predictable and she's getting bored.
- The romance reader feels there's no chemistry between your lead characters and they feel flat.
- The thriller reader feels the stakes are too low to make him care about the story.

The details of the comments might be off base, but they point to a problem that *does* exist. It's up to you to determine if the problem lies with the book not being the right type of book for that reader, or an issue you want to address.

Remember, not being the book a particular reader wants to read is not the fault of the manuscript.

On the flip side, you can still benefit from critiques outside your genre. *Would* a little mystery add humor or tension to your romantic comedy?

Maybe tension between the leads in your thriller is exactly what you need, only not the sexual kind. Perhaps a few scenes in your historical could benefit from a little excitement. It's fine to ignore advice that doesn't serve your story, but consider it first.

Trust your instincts to know when a comment is good for your book, bad for your book, or good, but not right for your book. Listen to what your critiquers *felt*, as well as what they said.

But (and this is a biggie)...

If you notice you ignore *a lot of* advice, you might want to examine why.

Are You Ignoring Advice That Can Help You?

Every writer gets at least one rough critique, and it's only natural to ignore words that hurt or sap your confidence. The danger comes when you consistently ignore the very advice that can help you just because it hurts or you don't like it. If you've been revising novel after novel (or the same novel multiple times) and don't think you're getting any better, step back, look at the situation objectively, and ask:

Are you getting the same advice from multiple sources? If a lot of the feedback says the same thing, there's something in the writing or story that needs fixing, especially if it's a larger issue that crops up no matter what piece you're working on. That suggests it's a skill problem, not an individual story problem.

Is the amount or quality of feedback you're getting declining? It's frustrating to spend a lot of time critiquing someone's work, only to have that advice ignored time and time again. People don't want to waste time on writers who brush them off and keep making the same mistakes. If you used to get detailed critiques back, and now you're getting short summarized reviews, you might want to think about *why* no one is bothering to help anymore.

Do you feel as if you ought to do it, but you're blowing it off because "that's what editors are for"? It happens—writers think problems in their work will be fixed once they sell it, and their work only needs to be "good enough" to land an agent or an editor. Not true at all. The manuscript needs to be as perfect and as polished as you can make it *before* it goes to an agent or editor (and that goes double if you plan to self or indie publish).

With any critique, trust your writer's compass. Focus on the story and keep asking what will make it better. You might take a few side trips getting there, but you'll work it out eventually.

Revising Overly Revised Manuscripts (The Frankendraft)

A Frankendraft differs from a draft you know needs heavy revising. It's been cut and stitched together so many times the scenes no longer work together, and the story is either so deeply buried or so watered down that it doesn't make a whole lot of sense anymore.

In this session, the goal is to determine if you have a Frankendraft, and discuss options for what to do with it.

Often, there's not much you can do with a Frankendraft, so be prepared. Your objectivity is gone since so much of the story is in your head that you no longer notice it's not on the page. Sometimes, it's so terribly flawed that it's best to be merciful and pull the plug. But all hope is not lost, and you *can* take steps to bring this monster back to life.

Step One: Say Goodbye

Accept that the Frankendraft is dead and put the manuscript in a drawer. You created this mess by revising it over and over, and it's time to start fresh. Forget the text you already wrote and focus on the *story* you wanted to tell. Rewrite it from scratch in a clean file. No more editing. No more trying to make *this* manuscript work. Treat it as if it were a brand-new idea and run from there.

It's usually worth taking some time at this stage to brainstorm as if the novel you wrote never existed. Take another look at the idea, maybe run through some exercises to inspire the muse and get a different perspective (I suggest my book, *Plotting Your Novel: Ideas and Structure* to help you here).

Step Two: Trim the Fat

Decide what's needed in the story and what's not. What's the single most important goal in the plot? That's your core conflict.

Remember, you're looking for an achievable goal here, not a premise. Something tangible, not a vague concept, such as "the romance between so and so." Look for what the protagonist wants, such as, "Bob wants to win Jane's heart."

What events are *critical* to resolving that goal? If they weren't there, there would be no story. List those events, but no more than ten. Now revise with your core conflict and those plot points and get rid of everything else.

I strongly suggest doing an outline here, even if you're not an outliner by nature. It'll help you see if your plot is working and if you have all the right pieces to write a solid novel without writing the actual novel. If there are glaring holes or problems, they'll show up here.

Step Three: Kill Some Characters

Hard as this will be, eliminating characters will go a long way toward stripping out what's unnecessary. Who is the single most important character in the story (that's your protagonist)? Who is their antagonist? Now get rid of everyone else (don't panic, you'll add some back!).

Make a list of all the other characters. Go through the list and ask if the two critical characters (protagonist and antagonist) absolutely totally need that person to resolve the story goal. It's okay to have a "maybe" list here, as you'll need some minor characters down the road.

REVISION RED FLAG: Watch out for "zombie" characters who might turn this draft back into a Frankendraft—look for anyone who brings a serious subplot with them. If their story risks overshadowing or hijacking the core conflict, they do not need to be there. Save them for their own novel, or cut that subplot out. In most cases, it's better to cut the character as well, so you're not tempted to return to that subplot.

Step Four: Go Five for Five

What are the five critical events that have to happen to resolve the core conflict? Who are the five (or fewer) critical characters necessary to achieve those goals?

Take those five plot events and spread them out over the course of the novel. Which one is the best starting place? One of the critical events in your story should be the inciting event. If it's not, go back to step four and try again. Which one is the ending? You should have figured out this event from step two.

Now, of the remaining three events, which one is the best midpoint reversal event? It should be large enough to sustain your middle, and interesting enough to keep readers guessing. (A midpoint reversal is something that happens in the middle of the novel to surprise readers or change how the story unfolds. It also gives you something to plot toward from the beginning, then deal with in a way that gets you to the ending).

Finally, take each of the two remaining events and put one on either side of the midpoint. These might make good first and second act endings.

You might say, "But I can't do that because the chronology is off now!" but don't worry about that. Just organize and look at those turning points. Is there a way to rework the chronology so that these events fall in that order? Forget what you *already* wrote. Don't try to slip in details you remember you like.

Look at the first event and determine a way to get to the second. Then to the third, and so on. Brainstorm. Think outside the box and imagine what your characters would do. These notes can be rough and sketchy—just try to get an idea of how *this* book can play out.

Those who have trouble plotting might get snagged here, so if you're not sure what to do, try a shift toward the characters and write out their front story. What are their roles in the novel? What do they do? How do they help? Follow their character journeys as if the novel were their story and see what happens. After that, look back and see where this journey overlaps the core conflict and where the plot points might occur.

You'll have a much tighter story and a clearer look at how that story might unfold. You can always add in more scenes or turning points to flesh it out, but be wary of sewing dead pieces back on and creating another Frankendraft. The goal here is to start fresh and breathe new life into the story, not fix the old manuscript.

Most times you have to bury a Frankendraft to keep it away from the villagers, but once in a while, you *can* save it and turn it into something wonderful.

Dealing With Multiple Drafts During a Revision

Some manuscripts go through several drafts before you find the best way to tell your story. Problem is, you can end up with multiple drafts containing good writing in every one. Finding a way to piece together all the best parts and still tell a cohesive story can be a challenge—and risks creating a Frankendraft.

In this session, the goal is to find the most effective way to manage multiple drafts during a revision.

Lists can be incredibly helpful at giving you an overall look at your novel, especially if it's in several pieces. Start figuring out which pieces contribute to your core conflict and which don't. You can hit the critical details in all the scenes you plan to use and see how they flow together. Maybe even use that one-line summary that describes the plot so you can see how they connect to the overall story arcs.

It can also help to create a new file and start pasting in all the scenes you want in the order you want them in. The story won't make a ton of sense since the scenes will likely be disjointed, but they'll be in place and give you a sense of how they flow and work together (and let you see where you might need to write more or cut back). For those using the Three Act Structure, this is quite helpful in determining where your major set pieces fall, and if the right scenes are in the right places. You might find you have too much setup in Act One and not enough scenes for Act Three (or vice versa), and will need to adjust.

Rethink Your Darlings

In multiple drafts, you'll likely have favorite moments you want to include, and you'll probably work hard to get them to fit. But just because it's a great scene doesn't mean it belongs in the final story or plot. Difficult-to-place scenes might not be the right scenes for the book. Forcing a scene can create a stumbling block for readers—it doesn't flow, it doesn't quite make sense, it doesn't advance the story.

This doesn't hold true for every tough bit to fit, and once in a while, you come up with a seriously cool way to make it work that you wouldn't have thought about otherwise. But if you find yourself beating your head against a scene, it might be time to file it away and save it for another story. Look at those favorite scenes and ask:

Does it advance the core conflict? No matter how good the scene is on its own, if it's not advancing the plot, it probably doesn't need to be there.

Does it offer new and relevant information? Often, a favorite scene is similar to one already in the manuscript. The idea appeals to you, and you write it multiple times or multiple ways. It's a good scene, sure, but it does nothing new.

Beware of Revision Smudge

Revision smudge is those bits and pieces left behind that reference something no longer in the story. Maybe you switched which characters were in the scene with your protagonist, or you changed a location of scene, or a goal shifted slightly and the stakes were altered. Reading these scenes feels right, but when you look closely, you realize the details refer to a part of the story that is no longer there. That reference was cut, changed, or moved to a new location. Some things to keep an eye out for:

- Are there any leftover names or details that don't belong?
- Is anything referenced that is no longer there, or has changed?
- Are there extra characters in a scene who aren't anywhere else in the story?
- Is the information revealed new, or has it been added elsewhere?

Check for Repeated Information

Repeated description and backstory often cause trouble when merging multiple drafts. A scene that originally introduced a character in chapter two might now be in chapter five, and readers already know that character by that time.

To help fix out-of-order or repeated details, search for each character's name (or a key detail of backstory) and verify where you revealed it first, then check if it was also mentioned any other place. This can be time consuming, but by the end, you'll know exactly where you wrote what about a character.

Revise Chronologically

Revising chronologically also helps see the story as it unfolds, since you can easily flip back and double check details. Even better, having just read it, the text will be fresh in your mind. You might even make an easy-to-check list of details you changed that need to be edited overall.

Piecing together multiple drafts can be tricky, but a little planning can save you a lot of time and effort, and direct you to the right areas to spend additional time on during your revision.

Workshop One: Revision Prep

The Goal of This Workshop: To organize your thoughts, analyze the manuscript's needs, and determine what revisions you want to do with this manuscript.

What We'll Discuss in This Workshop: How to evaluate a manuscript and determine what it needs, how to create editorial and character arc maps, and how to create a revision plan.

Welcome to Workshop One: Revision Prep

Before diving into a revision, it helps to know what you're working with and what shape your manuscript is in. Novels often change during a first draft, so any outlines or summaries could be outdated by the time you're ready to revise. Your goals for the novel might have changed as well, or even the direction you originally planned to take. Scheduling a day or two to take stock of what you've written and how that compares to your original vision can save you time and effort later.

It's tempting to skip these steps and dive right into the revision, but with all the work that goes into a draft, it's worth the extra effort to understand what you want from your revisions, and the best way you can accomplish your goals.

Take a Look at the Big Picture

You had an idea for this novel when you started it—a vision for what you wanted it to be. Maybe you never wavered from that path and the first draft is exactly what you expected it to be, but often the story changed and evolved as you wrote it. New ideas excited you and your original plan isn't so clear. You need a little reminder as to why you wrote this novel in the first place, and who you wrote it for.

In this session, the goal is to clarify what you want your novel to be.

Step One: What Do You Want This Novel to Be?

This may seem like a simple question, but it's more than "a YA fantasy" or "a futuristic thriller." Do you want it to be funny? Scary? Romantic? Do you want it to fall into a certain genre or subgenre? This is important if you plan to submit it to agents or publishers. Do you want it to entertain or do you want readers to think deeper thoughts? If so, what thoughts?

What type of novel you want to create will help guide you on what aspects to revise, whether it's adding humor, romance, tightening the pacing, raising the tension, or something more fundamental. A character-driven literary novel requires different elements than a hard-core thriller. Just as you wouldn't write them the same, you wouldn't revise them the same. Think of it like adding spice to a meal—you want to bring out the right flavors in your story.

REVISION RED FLAG: If you're not sure of the tone, style, or even genre you're aiming for, or you have multiple (and conflicting) tones and styles, that could indicate you haven't decided what type of novel this is yet. Try exploring the different genres your novel might fall into. Is the core conflict of your novel clear? Does it contain the common elements for any given genre or subgenre? Are the tone and mood consistent with your chosen genre?

Step Two: What Story Are You Telling?

You have a core story about something that intrigues you as a writer, perhaps even a general theme. What core idea is at the heart of your story? What themes are running through it? Forget plot, forget characters, forget details specific to the plot. Think about the general underlying story—at its heart, what is it?

That heart will be the unifying force tying your entire novel together (and often the theme). It will give the overall novel cohesiveness and make it about more than just the plot. Finding your core idea will give you a story compass that will guide you as you revise.

REVISION RED FLAG: If you have no theme or greater concept, don't fret. Not every novel has a theme or poses a greater, universal question. But it *is* an opportunity to make your novel stronger, so it's worth considering how a theme might improve your story. Are there common elements to your story that might further tie the plots or characters together? Is there a greater message beyond the "protagonist solves problem" aspect of the plot?

Step Three: Who is This Novel For?

We like to think our books appeal to "everyone who loves to read," but sadly, that's not true. Readers have their own likes and dislikes, and the better you understand your readers, the better your chances at giving them a book they'll love. Trying to be all things to all readers results in a mishmash of *bleh* that doesn't satisfy anyone.

Your intended audience has varied tastes and needs, and what a middle-grade-adventure lover wants to read is different from what a political-thriller reader wants. If your reader wants a fast pace, you'd want to revise to raise the stakes or tension, cut the fat, maybe add more hooks. If your reader is looking for more word pictures or inner journeys, you might revise to elaborate on your descriptions and character arcs, and build deeper emotions that connect readers more strongly to the characters.

Readers also expect to see elements common to a novel *of* that genre. Knowing those tropes helps you tailor your novel so it satisfies readers looking to read a good tale in their chosen genre.

REVISION RED FLAG: If you can't identify a basic target reader, that could indicate you're not sure where your novel belongs in the market or who it's for. While this isn't always a problem, it can make it hard to revise, because there's no clear direction of what the novel should be. Is it a mystery with romantic elements or a romance with a mystery? Each story appeals to a different type of reader and requires different revision paths. What type of reader is this novel trying to attract? Who do you see reading it?

Once you've clarified the type of novel you want yours to be, you'll have a better idea of what aspects of your manuscript you want to develop and what can be trimmed. You're now ready to examine your manuscript more closely and identify exactly what's in it and how it unfolds.

Create an Editorial Map

Even if you're a fast drafter and completed a manuscript in a few weeks, odds are you don't remember everything that happens in every scene. Without a clear understanding of what's in your novel, it's harder to know the best way to revise. Doing an editorial map (also called an edit map or book map) lets you know exactly how the novel unfolds and where it needs tweaking. It's also a handy reference tool when you need to check when or how something happens and don't want to search the entire manuscript.

In this session, the goal is to map out what happens in your novel to create an easy reference guide for your revision.

As you create your editorial map, keep an eye out for weak spots and scenes you want to work on later. Add revision notes at the end of your scene summaries, such as: "Needs stronger goal," or "Fix character arc." This can make it easier to organize your thoughts for more productive revision sessions.

Please note that this map is to determine what happens when, so don't worry if the plot events don't line up with a particular structure or template. If that's your goal for the revision, you'll fix it during the plot and structure sessions.

How to Create an Editorial Map

Go scene by scene and summarize the important aspects of the novel.

Step One: Identify What Happens in Every Scene or Chapter

Determine what happens in each scene, especially the plot-driving goals and conflicts, as these elements create the novel's plot. You can either list them or just think about them at first (we'll summarize next). If plot mechanics are a common weak area for your first drafts, I recommend listing the goals and motivations of each scene. It'll force you to be specific, and the act of writing them down crystallizes your intent, especially if you have trouble articulating what a scene is about or the goals driving it. Ask:

- What is the point-of-view character trying to do in this scene? (the goal)

- Why is she trying to do it? (the motivation for that goal)

- What's in the way of her doing it? (the conflict and scene obstacle)

- What happens if she doesn't do it? (the stakes)

- What goes wrong (or right)? (how the story moves forward)

- What important plot or story elements are in the scene? (what you need to remember or what affects future scenes.)

REVISION RED FLAG: If you're unable to answer any of these questions, that could indicate you're missing some of the goal-conflict-stakes plot mechanics. Make note of these areas, as you'll want to return to them later when it's time to strengthening these elements.

Step Two: Summarize What Happens in Every Scene or Chapter

Once you identify the core elements of the scene, summarize what happens—the actions and choices made. This will be a huge help in analyzing the novel's narrative drive and pacing.

REVISION RED FLAG: If you can't summarize the action in the scene, that could indicate there's not enough external character activity going on. Perhaps this scene has a lot of backstory, description, or infodumps in it. Be wary if there's a lot of thinking, but no action taken as a result of that thinking. Make notes on ways to add the character's goal back in, or how to possibly combine the scene with one that's weak on internal action.

Step Three: Map Out the Entire Novel

Go scene by scene and summarize the novel. By the end, you'll have a solid map of how the novel unfolds and what the critical plot elements are. You'll easily see where/if a plot thread dead ends or wanders off, or any scenes that lack goals or conflict.

REVISION RED FLAG: If you discover some chapters or scenes have a lot of information, while others have a line or two, that could indicate scenes that need fleshing out, or are heavy with non-story-driving elements that might need pruning. It could even show places where *too* much is going on and readers might need a breather. Mark the areas that need work, adding any ideas that might have occurred to you as you wrote your summaries.

REVISION TIP: *Try highlighting your notes in different colors to denote different elements, such as green for goals, red for tension. That makes it easy to skim over your editorial map and see where and what the weak spots are.*

Revision Option: Make Notes for Later

Get a head start by taking additional notes on elements you'll look at later. Some things worth identifying:

Story questions per scene or chapter: Look for the elements readers will wonder about.

Reveals of secrets or key information: When do characters discover important information? When do readers?

Key moments in any subplots: Add a line or two that shows any subplots and how they unfold. It's also useful to note how they connect to the main plot.

Revision Option: Map Out Any Additional Arcs You Might Want

Aside from the core plot elements, you can also include the pacing of reveals, discovery of clues or secrets, how multiple points of view affect each other, or whatever else you want to track. For example, a mystery might have one paragraph per chapter that covers what the killer is doing, even though that's never shown in the novel.

These additional details can be woven into the scene summary or kept as bullet points or a subparagraph if that's easier. You might even have two or three paragraphs per scene: One for the plot, one for the character arcs, and one for information *you* need, but the characters don't know yet.

This additional information is useful for tracking subplots or inner conflicts, as well as critical clues or what the antagonist is doing off-screen that's affecting the protagonist. Timelines can also appear here if you need to know when events happen to ensure everything works together and you don't have any twenty-seven-hour days. Try adding a simple time reminder at the top of every scene, such as: Day One, Morning.

REVISION RED FLAG: If you discover you have no other arcs, that could indicate there's not enough happening in your novel. A lack of plot could mean you have too many non-story elements bogging down the novel, such as an overload of description, too much world building, heavy infodumps or even an excess of internalization. It could also indicate a repetition of too-similar scenes, creating a plot that feels as though it moves forward, but it's the same basic scene goal and stakes repeated in multiple ways.

The beauty of an editorial map is that once the hard work is done and you have it all mapped out, it's a solid guide to the novel. If you get stuck during revisions you can open it up, see what happens when, clarify where the story needs to go, and get back on track.

Now that your editorial map is done and the novel is clear in your mind, it's time to see how the protagonist's character arc is unfolding.

Create a Character Arc Map

Some novels have strong character arcs (such as a character-driven story about a single person), while others have characters who barely arc at all (such as a plot-driven series). Whichever side your novel falls on, there should be *some* kind of change for the protagonist after going through the experience of the novel. If not, that's a red flag that the plot events don't matter to the life of the protagonist. She's no different at the end of the story versus the beginning.

In this session, the goal is to map out how your characters emotionally change over the course of the novel and create a guide for your character arcs and emotional turning points.

As you create your character arc map, keep an eye out for how your protagonist changes or grows over the course of the novel and where she changes. You don't have to develop a strong character arc if it would hurt your novel, but consider how much a basic arc will benefit the story. You can also develop character arcs for other characters if you wish.

How to Create a Character Arc Map

Step One: Identify the Scenes That Show Who the Protagonist is and/or How That Character Changes

Determine which scenes show important aspects of the protagonist's personality or key moments in her life, especially the events that force a change in views or beliefs. You can either list them or just think about them at first (we'll summarize next).

If character growth is a common weak area for your first drafts, try listing the motivations of each decision that causes change to clarify what's triggering that growth (positive or negative). It'll force you to be specific, and the act of writing it down crystallizes how that character grows, especially if you have trouble articulating why a character suddenly changes her ways. Some things to ask:

- What type of person is the character at the start of the novel?
- What type of person is the character at the end of the novel?

- What happens to create this change?
- When did these revelations or changes in behavior occur in the novel?
- What does the character believe at the start of the novel?
- What is believed by the end of the novel?
- What brings about this change in view?
- What is the character hiding (or what is hidden from her) at the start of the novel?
- What is revealed by the end of the novel?
- What emotional sacrifices are made over the course of the novel?

REVISION RED FLAG: If you're unable to answer many of these questions, that could indicate you're missing some of the motivations or reasons for character change. Make note of any unanswered questions, as you'll want to return to them later when it's time to strengthen these elements.

Step Two: Summarize How the Growth or Change Occurs

Once you've identified the key growth moments of the novel, summarize what happens in those scenes—the choices made and how they affect the protagonist. Aim for showing the direct steps that transform the character from who she is on page one to who she becomes by the last page.

REVISION RED FLAG: If you can't summarize why a character makes a choice that changes her, that could indicate there's not enough motivation or plausible reasons behind the change. Be wary if the change is significant and affects the plot but has no solid groundwork leading up to that change. Make notes on ways to strengthen the motives or add reasons for the character to act in a life-changing way.

Step Three: Map Out the Character Arc

Go scene by scene and summarize the protagonist's character arc in the novel. By the end, you'll have a solid map of where and how the character grows and changes, and what causes those changes. You'll see where/if the character changes for no reason, or where the reasons for the change required feel weak.

🚩 **REVISION RED FLAG:** If you notice most of the changes occur in the last act or around the climax of the novel, that indicates there's not enough growth occurring, and the character is changing because it's *time* to change. Also be wary of any areas where a lot of growth happens in a short amount of time, as this might indicate weak or missing motivations. Mark the scenes that need further development, adding any ideas that might have occurred to you as you did your summaries.

Revision Option: Map Out Any Additional Character Arcs Needed

Depending on how many characters you have, or who is important enough to grow, you might have other arcs to track. Map out the change moments for any additional characters you want to evolve in the novel. For example, you might want to track the love interest arc, or the best friend, or the antagonist. Even if the arcs are small or just show a change in attitude, views, or beliefs, characters who grow bring depth and texture to a story.

These arcs can also come in handy to fill holes or slow moments in the plot, or layer in extra tension where needed.

🚩 **REVISION RED FLAG:** If you discover no other character grows, that could indicate that the supporting characters do nothing but supply information or aid to the protagonist—and often, these characters seem flat because they have no lives of their own.

A character arc map is useful for referencing when, why, and how characters change over the course of the novel. Braiding the character arcs with the plot help ensure that something interesting (and story-moving) is happening in every scene.

Now that you've finished your editorial and character arc maps, analyze what's working in the overall novel and what still needs work.

Analyze the Draft

After doing your editorial and character arc maps, you should have a general idea of where the manuscript is weak and what you'd like to do to make it stronger. Use your maps as guides and conduct a more detailed analysis to pinpoint the areas to focus on.

In this session, the goal is to get a solid overview of where the weak spots lie in your novel, and provide you with the best guide to revise those issues.

If your first draft is clean and the plot is working, you might be ready to revise after doing the editorial and character arc maps (if so, you can skip this session). If the manuscript needs more attention, spend some time analyzing its strengths and weakness and decide what will best serve your story and help turn your manuscript into a nice, healthy novel.

You don't need to fix the problems now—this analysis is for identifying problem areas and directing your revision. Once you know what's weak or missing, you can devote more attention to the workshops aimed at those areas.

Things to look for (potential issues include, but are not limited to):

▶ **Weak goal-conflict-stakes structures:** This could indicate a plot or narrative drive issue.

▶ **Lack of character motivation:** This could indicate a character arc or credibility issue.

▶ **Sparse or missing descriptions:** This could indicate a clarity or world-building issue.

▶ **Heavy (or missing) backstory:** This could indicate a pacing or character issue.

▶ **Too many infodumps:** This could indicate a pacing or show-don't-tell issue.

▶ **Slow or uneven pacing:** This could indicate a narrative drive or pacing issue.

▶ **Lack of hooks:** This could indicate a tension, narrative drive, or premise issue.

▶ **Faulty logic:** This could indicate a plausibility or plotting issue.

▶ **Weak or missing foreshadowing or clues:** This could indicate a tension, tone, or description issue.

▶ **Areas that need more emotion:** This could indicate an internalization issue.

▶ **Weak characters and character arcs:** This could indicate a character or internal conflict issue.

▶ **Weak scene structure:** This could indicate a plot or structure issue.

▶ **Lack of narrative drive:** This could indicate a pacing or goals issue.

▶ **Inconsistent point of view:** This could indicate a narrative, character, or show-don't-tell issue.

▶ **Weak dialogue:** This could indicate an infodump, dialogue, or character issue.

If you're unsure what specifically to look for, try answering these questions (be as objective as possible):

▶ Is the point-of-view character(s) likable or interesting enough to read about?

▶ Are their goals clear so there's narrative drive in the story?

▶ Do the characters seem real?

▶ Are there strong and interesting stakes?

▶ Is there too much back story, exposition, or description?

▶ Is the overall structure holding together?

▶ Does the opening scene have something to entice readers to keep reading?

▶ Do the scene and chapter endings entice readers to turn the page?

▶ Is the pacing strong?

▶ Are the plots, stakes, and goals believable?

▶ Does it read well overall?

▶ Do the sentences flow seamlessly or do any stick out and read awkwardly?

▶ Are the dialogue tags clear?

▶ Does the world seem fleshed out?

After the analysis, you should have a good idea of what areas need work. The next step is organizing your notes into a solid revision plan.

Create a Revision Plan

A revision plan helps you get a head start on what you know you want to revise so you're not spending time later deciding what to do. It's a good way to organize your thoughts and look at the overall project before you start, giving you a chance to spot any pitfalls before you stumble into them.

It's easy to get caught up in the story, or worse, chase a new shiny idea that mucks up the novel. The story can, of course, change as you revise, but a revision plan can give you that extra layer of protection against adding more because it's new versus developing what's already written.

In this session, the goal is to help you organize your thoughts and create a plan to revise your novel in the most effective way.

If you made enough notes in the previous steps and feel confident about your revision goals, you can skip this and move on to the next workshop. If you want more organization or guidance on how to approach the revision, continue with step one.

Step One: Condense Any Feedback or Critique Notes

If you sent the manuscript out for critique, read through the feedback you received and make notes of what you'd like to address. Perhaps highlight or copy into a notes file anything that requires broad strokes to fix—such as reworking a scene or changing something on a macro level.

It's also helpful to copy line comments directly into the manuscript so you have everything in one file, especially if you receive several different comments on the same scene. This could point to a slightly different problem somewhere else that your readers are picking up on.

Also review any notes you might have made on elements you want to change. The goal is to get your thoughts and feedback into one place so you can easily review it.

Step Two: Make Notes on Any Revisions You Want in Each Scene

Break out your editorial map and scan though each scene. Look for any notes or comments you made on known problems or aspects you want to work on. Add any feedback from your critique notes, and anything you noted during your manuscript analysis.

Putting these notes in a different color can help immediately identify what to do with each scene. It's also helpful to write out what needs to be revised or added in the scene summary, such as:

> Just as Bob thinks he's zombie breakfast, Sally rushes in with her gun (does it make sense she'd do this?) and shoots the zombie. It has little effect, but does distract it long enough for Bob to get a few inches out of biting range. He yells to go for the head and Sally does, killing the zombie. Bob is happy to be alive, and then panics when he remembers Jane is all alone at the office with these things on the loose (make sure his emotional shift is logical). He has to get to her. Sally takes in the scene and starts yelling at Bob for his poor choice in weaponry and what was he thinking? (Layer in subtext that relates to their failing marriage.) He's just about to lay into her when they hear more moaning from outside. A lot more. (Could this "need to tell her off" be part of his inner arc?)

If this style doesn't appeal to you, take notes in whatever format works for you. If it helps, summarize what needs to be done in each scene, chapter, and/or the entire manuscript.

Even small reminders of problem areas will make it easier to find and fix these areas.

Step Three: Plan Your Approach

Once you know what you want to do, decide how you want to approach your revision. Are you a one-chapter-at-a-time writer who likes to get that chapter perfect before moving forward? Or maybe you prefer one item at a time, such as checking for goals in the entire novel, then looking at description, then looking for trouble words? Maybe you're more of a large chunk of several chapters at a time reviser and like to get one act done before moving to the next. However you prefer to revise, knowing what you'll work on each session keeps you focused.

Step Four: Make Your Revisions

Some edits are easy to do—fixing the typos, changing a name or term, clarifying an ambiguous pronoun. If you need a little warm up before you get to the tough edits, do these first—they take the least amount of brain power and offer a sense of accomplishment. Momentum helps a lot in a revision.

Some revision passes work better when you look at the entire manuscript vs. smaller chunks, so feel free to vary how you review your manuscript. For example, continuity checks are harder to do in chunks, since you might forget what happened between reads. Reading the manuscript in a short timeframe keeps the details fresh in your mind and makes it easier to spot where something is off.

After you're done, re-read your notes and critiques to see if you've addressed everything you wanted to. Double check any feedback that you ignored to see if you have a new opinion on it now (it happens). Tweak as needed.

Step Five: Gain Some Perspective

Once the revision is done, schedule some downtime so the manuscript can sit for a while and the details can fade from your memory. I like to give it a month, but aim for at least a week, longer if the changes were extensive. You want to give your brain time to forget what *was* there so when you look at it again, you'll see what *is* there. There's always some revision smudge that slips into the text that refers to something that changed or was cut.

When you're ready, read through the manuscript once more and make any changes that jump out. Most of it will likely be small edits, a word change here and there. It's not uncommon to cut sentences or even paragraphs that slow the story down now that you've been away and can spot the dead weight. However, if you're still making large changes and rewriting sections, you might consider going back to step four and reworking those trouble spots.

Step Five: Polish the Manuscript

After the story is as good as you can make it, it's time to polish the text until it shines. This is where you'll address individual word choices, copyedits, and grammar goofs you might have made. These elements don't affect the story, but focus on the technical aspects of writing.

Don't be afraid to mix it up or change the order of these steps if that works for you. Some folks might prefer to do the larger issues first and finish up with the easy edits and that's okay. The whole goal of a revision plan is to keep you focused and provide a way to track your progress.

Now that you've refreshed the intricacies of your story in your mind, and planned out what needs tweaking and how you want to approach it, it's time to move on to the manuscript itself.

This book is all about the plot, so let's examine your plot and structure first.

Workshop Two:
Plot and Structure Work

The Goal of This Workshop: To strengthen and clarify your plot, story structure, and narrative drive.

What We'll Discuss in This Workshop: Ways to analyze your plot, story structure, and narrative drive, and ways to fix any issues found during the analysis.

Welcome to Workshop Two:
Plot and Structure Work

Stories are about interesting people, solving interesting problems, in interesting ways. Workshop Two covered the interesting people, so now let's look at the interesting problems and the ways your characters solve those problems.

Plot and structure work together to create the foundation for your story to flourish, giving it the support and guidance it needs. It's also where a lot of common first-draft problems surface, because a good plot requires you to think on your feet, be original, and constantly surprise your readers.

Your plot illustrates your story to your readers and lets your characters act. The plot is how they interact with each other and how they resolve the problems thrown at them in the novel.

The novel's structure provides the framework for the plot to unfold, while the individual scenes make up the plot, and the narrative drive ensures every piece flows smoothly (and compellingly) from one to the next.

Outliners (those who prefer to outline a story and know the details before they start writing) and plot-focused writers will likely be stronger in this area, while pantsers (those who prefer to dive in without knowing or planning their story) and character-focused writers will probably need to do more work here.

A good plot is like a well-crafted puzzle. Each piece is vital to the bigger picture, connecting to each other to tell the larger tale. Too many pieces are too hard to keep track of, too few create too simple a puzzle.

Analyze the Story Structure

No matter what structure you use, the general storytelling format remains the same. A protagonist discovers a problem, decides to solve that problem, has a hard time doing so, but eventually overcomes the obstacles and faces the antagonist in the end to resolve the problem. Key turning points exist in these moments, and this framework from beginning to end provides the structure for the novel. How you choose to develop that structure and story is up to you.

In this session, the goal is to examine your basic story structure for any missing or out of place turning points that might throw off the flow of the novel.

In the next sessions, we'll look at your plot and subplots, scene structure, narrative drive, tension, hooks.

A note about structure: As you go through these questions, keep in mind that the terms used are meant in a general, conceptual way. For example, the "final battle" doesn't have to be an actual battle, or even a fight; it's the final moment when the two conflicting sides (protagonist vs. antagonist) resolve the conflict.

Determine if the Story Structure is Working

What makes story structure so valuable is that it provides solid, proven turning points that can help you decide what events need to happen when to get the most out of your stories. It also helps you find holes in the plot, and places where the stakes might need to be raised.

Grab your editorial map and look at the novel as a whole. Ask:

▶ **Are all the pieces in the right places?** Key turning points in the plot keep the story moving forward. Put the right piece in the wrong turning point, and the novel can drag, or feel rushed if events happen too early.

▶ **Does the opening scene present an intriguing problem or mystery to draw readers in?** The goal of the opening scene is to pique readers' interest and make them want to read on. Is there something interesting happening on page one that makes you want to read page two?

▶ **Is there an inciting event within the first thirty pages (or fifty pages for longer manuscripts) that puts the protagonist on the path to the rest of the novel?** In every story there's a moment early on that changes the protagonist's life forever by putting her on the plot path—if it hadn't happened, the plot wouldn't unfold as it does and the story wouldn't have happened.

▶ **Is there a moment in the beginning where the protagonist makes the *choice* to pursue the story problem?** Near the end of the beginning (around the 25 percent mark in a traditional Three Act Structure), the protagonist has the option of saying "no" and not pursuing the core conflict goal, but makes a choice to move ahead with the plot and venture into the unknown.

▶ **Do the stakes escalate at this time?** Good story structure provides opportunities for the stakes to escalate at major turning points of the plot.

▶ **Does something happen in the middle of the book that changes how the story problem is viewed or approached?** The middle of the book often gets harder for the protagonist and plans start to fall apart—whether she realizes it or not. Or truths might be revealed which change how the entire story thus far has been viewed or understood.

▸ **Are the stakes raised again around this time?** Stakes typically become more personal and the risks get higher at the midpoint, and the protagonist is now more invested in resolving the problem.

▸ **Is there a dark moment or setback right before the ending starts that raises the stakes again?** As obstacles get tougher for the protagonist, it becomes uncertain if she can win. Shortly before the ending (around the 75 percent mark in the Three Act Structure) everything is (or has been) stripped away, and the protagonist loses all hope and doesn't see a way out of the problem.

▸ **Are the stakes raised yet again?** Often, this is when the highest, most personal stakes come into play—an all or nothing, do or die consequence.

▸ **Does the protagonist make the decision to continue the fight despite the risks or sacrifices?** This is a critical moment that triggers the climax, sending the protagonist to face off against the antagonist to resolve the novel's core conflict.

▸ **Is there a clear win for the protagonist at the climax? Something that must be done in order to succeed?** The final battle uses everything the protagonist has learned so far, and what must be done to win is clear (though *how* is often still a mystery).

▸ **Does the ending resolve itself in a way that satisfies the story questions posed in the beginning of the novel?** Not every loose end needs to be tied up, but the core conflict and the major plot threads should be answered to reader satisfaction.

▸ **Is the ending satisfying?** A satisfying ending equates to a satisfying novel, since it's the last thing readers see. It's the ending readers have been waiting for, and it gives them what they wanted—though not always in the way they expect.

REVISION RED FLAG: If you're missing any of these points, that could indicate the structure is off or out of alignment, and a critical plot moment is still needed.

Problems Found?

If you think your story structure needs adjusting, try the exercises in If You Want to Adjust Your Story Structure on page 63.

Analyze the Plot and Subplots

Every scene in your novel should move the story forward, building on the individual goals to resolve a conflict, which in turn forms a cohesive story. Plot isn't a series of dramatized moments from someone's life, but characters making choices and acting in ways that affect them and others.

In this session, the goal is to analyze the plot and subplots to make sure they're advancing the story through solid goals, clear motivations, strong conflicts, and high stakes.

In the next sessions, you'll look at your scene structure, narrative drive, tension, and hooks.

Step One: Determine if the Plot is Working

With so many moving parts, plotting can be a tough element to analyze, especially when every plot is different. Trust your writer's instinct and let it guide you during your analysis.

▶ **Does the plot make sense?** Confusion is never good in a story, and it's one of the harder aspects to check in your own writing—you *know* what it all means. If you *didn't* know how these events all interconnected, would it make sense? Do you need to explain anything for others to understand it?

▶ **Is there a clear core conflict driving the plot?** It should be clear by the end of the beginning (Act One if you use the Three Act Structure) what the main problem of the novel is, even if some details are still a mystery.

▶ **Are the characters' actions believable?** A quick way to lose readers is to have characters behave in ways that strain credibility. Check if your plots feel unrealistic, contrived, or coincidental. Make sure it makes sense for the characters to be doing whatever they need to do in the novel.

▶ **Was the plot predictable?** No matter how well-written a novel, predictability will hurt it. If readers can see what's coming long before it happens, there's no reason to keep reading. Do events turn out exactly how anyone would expect them to? Are there enough twists and turns to keep readers guessing?

▶ **How often does the protagonist have to make a choice?** Choices drive a plot. If the protagonist isn't making a lot of decisions and is just going along with whatever happens, that indicates a reactive protagonist and a plot with no goals, conflicts, or stakes.

▶ **Are those choices difficult?** Easy choices aren't real choices and indicate a lack of true conflict in a scene. There should be consequences, both good *and* bad, with every choice the protagonist has to make. The bigger the turning point, the higher the cost, and the tougher the decision.

▶ **Does the protagonist have approaches different from the other characters' toward solving problems or looking at situations?** Different opinions about how to resolve the story's conflict make for more unpredictable plots. If everyone always agrees with the protagonist on how to proceed, that could indicate a predictable plot.

▶ **Are any leaps in logic or the decision-making process plausible?** Look for places where characters suddenly figure out an important clue or plot point without solid groundwork to back it up. It's not uncommon in a first draft for characters to "magically" know the answer to a problem even though they didn't earn it.

▶ **Do coincidences work to aid the protagonist instead of hindering her?** If so, that could indicate a lack of real conflict and no struggle to complete goals.

▶ **Are the protagonist's motivations plausible?** There should be reasons the protagonist is willing to risk something to resolve this problem. Look for any spots where the protagonist is acting only because the plot said so.

▶ **Is someone or something opposing the protagonist?** A weak antagonist often leads to weak plots, because there's no worthy foe trying to stop the protagonist.

▶ **Does the antagonist have a plan, or does he cause random trouble when the plot needs it?** If the plot feels a little random or coincidental, look at what the antagonist's plan is. If the actions aren't the result of *his* pursuit of *his* goal, he might be tossing pointless obstacles in the protagonist's way.

▶ **Is the antagonist trying to win, or does he sometimes act stupidly so the protagonist can win?** Look for any spots where the plot events hinge on the antagonist making a stupid mistake or acting like an idiot. The tougher—and smarter—your antagonist, the better the plot will be, because the protagonist's victories will be earned.

▶ **Do the choices create conflict between the protagonist's internal and external goals?** Strong plots put the protagonist's external goal at odds with the internal goal, creating difficult or impossible choices.

▶ **Is the protagonist asked or forced to do something that goes against her beliefs?** If beliefs are never tested or strained, that could indicate a weak character arc and a protagonist who doesn't grow or change.

▶ **Are there strong stakes?** Even when the protagonist has goals, without consequences for failure, they can seem flat and uninteresting. Check for consequences if the protagonist fails to get what she wants. Make sure what she wants matters, and not achieving that goal has serious repercussions.

▶ **Do the stakes escalate as the novel unfolds?** Problems should get worse and worse for the protagonist as she struggles to complete her goals. Look for places where the stakes never change, such as every scene having the same risk ("the protagonist's life is at risk" is a common non-escalating stakes issue). In essence, it's the classic "how can you make things worse?" question.

▶ **Will the protagonist's life change if she fails to achieve her goal?** Even if the change is small, every scene should affect the protagonist. If not, the scene can feel pointless and unnecessary.

▶ **Do the stakes affect the protagonist personally?** Sometimes the stakes seem high (such as the lives of thousands of people), but since they don't affect the *protagonist*, readers don't care.

▶ **Is it impossible for the protagonist to walk away from this problem?** If she can, that indicates the stakes aren't personal enough. Consider raising the stakes and making the consequences for failing harsher.

▶ **Are the stakes clear from the beginning of the novel?** Sometimes the stakes aren't obvious and the reasons behind a character's actions don't make sense. Look for places where your characters can discuss or consider the risks—even if you never plan to have them happen. It's the fear of what *could* happen that helps raise the stakes.

▶ **Are the stakes big enough to be worth the reader's time?** Someone can write the best book ever on a man choosing which sushi restaurant to dine at for lunch, but unless readers care about the consequence of that choice, they won't care about the character or the novel. Just having stakes isn't enough if the stakes are minor or inconsequential.

Problems Found?

If you find any plotting issues, spend some time doing the exercises in If You Want to Deepen the Plot on page 107.

Step Two: Determine if the Subplots Are Working

Subplots work with your plots to layer in complexity and emotional growth, shedding more light on different aspects of the characters, and showing deeper meaning to the plot events.

▶ **What's your goal (as the author) for the subplot?** If you're devoting time to this subplot, what do *you* want it to do? How will it enhance the novel?

▶ **Are the subplots contributing to the core conflict or character arc?** The role of a good subplot is to add layers and emotional depth to the story, often on a more personal level than the main plot. For example, a romance subplot is quite common, even in non-romance genres. Look for any subplots that feel extraneous to the core conflict and do nothing to enhance the story in any meaningful way.

▶ **Will this subplot make the story better, or just longer?** If all it does is delay the time it takes for the protagonist to complete her goal, it might not be a worthy subplot. It should affect something in the story, plot, or character arc, otherwise it's just "stuff" the protagonist has to slog through to get anywhere.

▶ **If you took the subplot out, what's lost?** Consider how the story would unfold without this subplot. What would be lost? What might be gained? Would it change the way readers see the story? Would it change the way the characters see the problem? If the protagonist or another major character won't be changed by *not* going through this experience, you probably don't need it.

▶ **Does it explore a new problem (and likely raise the stakes) or re-peat a similar scene or idea you've already done?** At the resolution of this subplot, will the protagonist be worse off than she was before, either internally or externally? Be wary if this subplot only shows yet *another* way the protagonist's life is threatened, or has the same stakes you've already established.

▶ **Does it require more attention (and words) than the main plot?** Often you start to question a subplot because it feels as if it's hijacking the story. If you're spending more time on it than on the core conflict, that's a red flag you might have the wrong main plot, or this subplot is too strong for this story.

▶ **Is your protagonist trying to do too much in too many subplots?** Having too many subplots can make it hard to know what the story is about. What does the protagonist learn or gain from solving this mini-problem (this might relate to the inner conflict or character arc), and how does it help solve (or make it harder to solve) the core conflict? If it doesn't do either, cut it.

▶ **Is the subplot compelling enough that readers won't mind the de-lay in getting back to the main goal, or will they think you're drag-ging your feet to keep making the problem worse?** If readers don't care about this subplot, they'll get bored and start skimming, won-dering when you'll get back to the real story. Make any side stories just as intriguing as the main plotline, and offer compelling story questions to keep readers invested in the novel.

Problems Found?

If you find any subplot issues, spend some time doing the exercises in If You Want to Deepen the Plot: Developing the Subplots on page 129.

Analyze the Scenes

Scenes are the relay racers of plot. Not only do they need to have their own goals, conflicts, and stakes, they need to build off a previous scene and hand off the story to the *next* scene. When they stumble, the entire plot can stumble.

In this session, the goal is to examine the individual scenes to make sure each one is contributing to the story as a whole.

In the next sessions, you'll see if the narrative drive is moving the story, and examine the level of tension and hooks.

Determine if the Scenes Are Working

Begin by looking at your editorial map. Start with scene one and go scene by scene to the end of the novel, pinpointing the plot-driving aspects of the scene. If plotting is a weak area for you, write these down. Being specific will make it clear when something is missing from a scene.

If the scenes are structurally sound, you should clearly see how they move the plot forward. Some scenes will take small steps, others will make giant leaps. Ask:

▶ **How does this scene serve the story?** Something in the scene should cause a change somewhere. Otherwise, the scene can feel pointless. Make sure each scene affects plot and story movement or reveals new information.

▶ **How does this scene serve the protagonist's character arc?** Not every scene will affect the growth of the protagonist, but be wary if you see few scenes affecting the character arc.

▶ **How does this scene serve the *other* characters' arcs?** It's not all about the protagonist. Sometimes the best way to serve the story is to let another character illustrate one part of it through actions, choices, or options. Even what the antagonist is doing can force your protagonist to consider different options that reflect your story.

▶ **Where does this scene take place?** The setting should be clear and benefit the scene somehow.

▶ **What is the point-of-view character trying to do?** The goal should be clear and the bulk of the scene should revolve around trying to achieve that goal.

▶ **What goes wrong? What's the problem or challenge?** The conflict should be clear, with enough obstacles or challenges to make the struggle to achieve it worthwhile, as well as uncertain.

▶ **Why is this important and how does it potentially hurt the point-of-view character?** The stakes should be clear and of high enough consequence to cause reader concern if the character fails.

▶ **Who else is in the scene?** Make sure readers know who's in the scene early on so the "sudden" appearance of a character doesn't throw them out of the story. This doesn't apply if the whole point was to shock them.

▶ **What happens right before this scene?** The previous scene should lead to this scene (opening scenes are exempt, of course). In multiple-point-of-view novels, the previous scene in that point of view is the most likely lead in.

▶ **What does the point-of-view character do next?** The scene should suggest where the plot needs to go and give the protagonist a new goal or task if the current goal is not met.

▶ **If you took any scenes out, would the plot change?** If nothing about the plot would change if a scene is cut, that indicates you don't need that scene, or it needs a reason to be there.

🚩 **REVISION RED FLAG:** Pay attention to scenes that feel aimless or slow, especially any scenes you wanted to skim (or did skim) while re-reading the manuscript. Wanting to skim a scene is an indication that it's uninteresting and not worth re-reading. It's also common to skim a scene because it feels "fine" and needs no work, but upon a later re-read, you discover it does have issues or doesn't need to be there. Also take a closer look at any scenes you think *need* to be there, even though your instincts say it's not the most interesting scene. There's a good chance there's necessary information there, and if you move it, that scene can go.

Problems Found?

If you find any scene issues, spend some time doing the exercises in If You Want to Develop the Scenes on page 140.

Analyze the Narrative Drive

Narrative drive is the force that moves the story from beginning to end. It makes the plot seem as though it's going somewhere and isn't a bunch of scenes wandering aimlessly looking for a point. A weak narrative drive leads to a story that rambles and a plot that encourages skimming.

In this session, the goal is to analyze the narrative drive to see if the story is advancing in a compelling way.

Your editorial map can be a good first step here and help you pinpoint larger trouble spots, but you should also do a scene-by-scene analysis.

Determine if the Narrative Drive is Working

Look at your novel and focus on the reasons readers will want to keep reading. Find the elements pulling them through the plot and keeping them hooked in the story. Ask:

▶ **Are the character and story goals clear so there's narrative drive in the story?** Plots are all about characters acting to achieve goals, and their actions should move the story forward. Even if the details are still a mystery, there should be a sense of a story unfolding toward a resolution.

▶ **Is the protagonist doing something in every scene?** A plot that moves forward has the protagonist trying to accomplish tasks, even if she fails.

▶ **Is there a story point (author's perspective) to every scene?** What are *your* reasons for a scene to be there? Look for the important elements that you wanted to show as the author.

▶ **Is there a story question (reader's perspective) in every scene?** Questions keep the story moving. Look for the puzzles readers will wonder about and want answers to.

▶ **Are these points and questions clear from the start of the scene?** Good narrative drive makes it clear where the story is going, even if the details are still unknown. Readers can see the plot is progressing, and there are still plenty of puzzles to solve.

▶ **Is the protagonist moving toward something?** If there's a lot of "stuff happening" *to* your protagonist, and not a lot of her *doing* anything, it could signal a reactive plot brewing. It might be a good idea to do a goal check and see what's driving the protagonist to act.

▶ **Do the scenes and chapters build on one another or are events happening one after another?** Scenes should affect other scenes or the story can feel episodic. Is the plot a cohesive story or a series of scenes stuck together? Does it have a point?

▶ **Where is the critical information revealed?** Information will be spoon fed to readers the entire book, but you'll usually find a handful of shocking plot twists, surprises, or big reveals in every novel. Where do your surprises and twists fall? Do any fall too close to another major plot point or character arc moment? If they're clumped together, perhaps space them out more to keep the tension high.

▶ **Is the protagonist feeling too much?** If your scenes focus more on emotions and not so much on action, you might be short on external goals. Look at the goals and make sure there's enough for the protagonist to do to keep the plot moving.

▶ **Is the protagonist debating too much?** If you have a lot of sections where the protagonist is figuring out information or debating what to do next, this could indicate not enough plot events. You might look for ways to get the protagonist moving and trying to accomplish tasks, *while* struggling with inner turmoil or figuring out a puzzle.

🚩 **REVISION RED FLAG:** Scenes that lack narrative drive often illustrate an aspect of the story or world, more like extended infodumps than plot-driving events. If you find the same basic goal, that could indicate nothing new is happening and the story might feel repetitive.

Problems Found?

If you find any issues with the narrative drive, spend some time doing the exercises in If You Want to Strengthen the Narrative Drive on page 147.

Analyze the Tension and Hooks

When a scene feels like nothing is happening even when you *know* things are, the most likely culprit is a lack of tension. The scene is predictable and readers can guess how it's going to turn out, even if they don't know the details. Adding hooks and increasing the tension will create a sense that something is about to happen, whether that's a plot turning point, a secret revealed, or an answer readers have been waiting for.

In this session, the goal is to examine your hooks and make sure there's enough tension to keep readers in the story.

Determine if the Hooks and Tension Are Working

Grab your editorial map or manuscript and look at how your scenes and chapters start and end. Identify the hooks meant to draw readers in, and the elements that will keep them reading. Ask:

▶ **Is there a sense of something about to happen in every scene?** There should be a sense of anticipation about something no matter what is going on. Look for places where you frequently skim or read quickly, as these are often where the slow, tension-weak areas lie.

▶ **Are there unanswered questions in every scene?** If you marked these on your editorial map, it should be easy to see what you have and where they fall. If not, look for places where you posed questions that still need to be answered.

▶ **Is there tension on every page?** Though time consuming to do, it's a good idea to go through the novel and make sure there's a sense of something being held back, something about to happen, or a potential problem brewing on every page.

▶ **Is there tension between characters?** There should be differences of opinion and problem-solving approaches. Look for tension-weak places where characters all agree.

▶ **Is there tension in the setting?** Inherent conflicts in the setting can create tension in a scene. Look for places where the setting isn't doing anything besides giving the scene a place to happen.

▶ **Are there moments when the protagonist is relaxed?** A relaxed protagonist is a big indication there's no tension in that scene.

▶ **Are there big reveals and discoveries throughout the novel?** Aim for a new discovery or reveal every chapter. It doesn't have to be huge, just something new. Also look for a solid arc between big moments that raise tension for the entire novel.

▶ **How many reveals are plot-related?** This can indicate pacing issues, as things are (or are not) happening to move the story along. Few plot reveals or discoveries suggest too many similar scenes or a novel that's episodic in nature.

▶ **How many reveals are character-related?** This indicates how the character growth arc or internal conflict is moving along. If the protagonist isn't learning or revealing new details about herself, she might not be growing. Few character reveals suggests nothing is changing about that character and she's not trying or learning new things.

▶ **How many reveals are backstory or world-building related?** If you have a lot here (or the balance is way off in favor of this), it's a red flag that your protagonist might not be driving the story. The focus is on telling the history of a place or person, not on what the characters are doing. Some backstory reveals are fine since readers will want to know that history if it bears on the plot or a character arc, but if a lot of the reveals or discoveries are "cool" aspects of the world or situation, it could mean you have a premise novel on your hands.

REVISION RED FLAG: Too many reveals at the start of the book often indicate too much backstory or exposition. Heavy reveals at the end could indicate a lack of discovery during the story, or that you're holding out on readers and not giving them enough reveals to keep them interested.

If You Want to Adjust the Story Structure

Stories have a beginning, a middle, and an ending—three points that frame a novel and offer a compelling tale to your readers. What you put into that frame can (and does) vary wildly, and you're not beholden to any one structure or format. Even if you love a particular structure, you have the freedom to vary it and adjust it to suit whatever story you're telling at the time.

In this session, the goal is to adjust any out-of-alignment structures, and make sure the story is unfolding in the strongest possible way.

You'll also explore common problems with beginnings, middles, and endings, and how to fix them.

Step One: Create a Structure Outline Template Using Your Preferred Outline

It's a good idea to get a sense of how the structure is working over-all and where the major turning points lie. Using your editorial map and your preferred structure format, write what happens at each of the major turning points of your novel (plotters and outliners will likely already have this in their files). These moments are typically external moments, with the protagonist acting to move the plot forward. Aim for at least a sentence or two that summarizes what happens.

REVISION RED FLAG: If you have a lot of "is told information" or "bad things happen *to* the protagonist" moments, that could indi-cate a reactive protagonist who's not driving the plot.

Don't Have a Structure Style?

If you don't have a preferred structure style, try using the classic Three Act Structure to start. It allows for plenty of flexibility while still pro-viding a solid framework on which to hang your plot. The Three Act Structure uses the following major turning points:

Act One: The Beginning (The first 25 percent of the novel)

Opening Scene: How the protagonist and world are introduced.

Inciting Event: When the protagonist is first pulled onto the plot path (typically occurs within the first 10 percent of the novel—somewhere in the first thirty or fifty pages for longer novels).

Act One Problem: When the protagonist first realizes there's a problem and must make a choice to move forward (typically occurs on or around the 25 percent mark of the novel).

Act Two: The Middle (The middle 50 percent of the novel)

Act Two Choice: When the protagonist makes a choice and decides to act (typically occurs right after the 25 percent mark of the novel).

Midpoint Reversal: When the situation unexpectedly changes (typi-cally occurs at or around the 50 percent mark of the novel).

Act Two Disaster: When the worst happens and the protagonist wants to give up (typically occurs at or around the 75 percent mark of the novel).

Act Three: The Ending (The last 25 percent of the novel)

Act Three Plan: When the protagonist decides to risk it all to fix the problem (typically occurs just after the 75 percent mark of the novel).

Climax: When the protagonist faces the antagonist and resolves the problem (typically occurs at or around the 90 percent mark of the novel).

Wrap Up: Where the protagonist goes from here (final scene of the novel).

Step Two: Move Scenes and Turning Points as Needed

Major plot turning points don't have to fit a template exactly, but structure is a proven way to craft stories for readers. It covers the natural rise and fall of stakes, pursuit of goals readers have come to expect from a novel.

Major plot events that fall way outside the general structure format usually indicate problems with the overall structure of the novel.

Be concerned if:

A turning point falls more than 20 percent outside the general range: This can indicate a pacing issue, or too much information in the story (infodumps, backstory, subplots, exposition, etc.). Variances of 10 percent are normal, but the farther it goes beyond that the more likely there's a problem.

A turning point is missing altogether: This can indicate a narrative drive or plotting problem. For example, if there's no Act One problem, then what transitions the protagonist from the beginning to the middle? Chances are the middle is bogging down or wandering because there's no clear goal driving it.

A turning point occurs in a different section: This can indicate a plot that's out of whack, with pacing and stakes issues, and likely a narrative drive issue. For example, if a typically high-stakes turning point occurs too early, the novel can peak long before tensions have time to build, leading to an anticlimactic ending.

Multiple turning points occur close together: This can indicate there's not enough plot to flesh out the entire novel, or it might have a pacing issue. Turning points work because they support the plot and story and allow for waves of tension and reveals to build over the course of the novel.

As you work through your structure, you might also discover a chapter, scene, or elements of a scene that fit better elsewhere. Reorganize the manuscript so it unfolds in the strongest way possible.

Structure holds a novel together and takes some of the guesswork out of revisions. If the structure is out of alignment, it throws off the entire story, but once you get it adjusted, what you need to do to strengthen your stories is much more clear.

Step Three: Fix Problems With the Beginning

Beginnings contain a lot of setup and introduction, so it's not uncommon for them to start off wrong, or take too much time to get going. If a beginning isn't working, it's usually due to not grabbing readers' interest, either by lack of a compelling problem, nothing happening to draw readers in, or taking too long to get to the story. For more in-depth discussions on these issues, see Fixing Common Problems With the Beginning on page 73.

Common beginning problems include:

Starting in the wrong place: If you're worried the novel is starting too soon, look for scenes where the protagonist is going through a lot of normal day routines without a goal, conflict, or problem. In too-late beginnings, look for a lot of action and characters in dire straits without a clear reason, sense of who they are, or context for what's going on.

Too much (or not enough) setup: Too much setup results in slow beginnings full of infodumps, backstory, and too much setting the scene to "get readers ready" for the story to start. Not enough setup leads to confusing beginnings that lack enough information and ramp up for readers to understand what's happening and why it matters.

Lack of story questions: Beginnings that aren't grabbing readers often lack hooks or narrative drive. Things may be happening, but nothing makes readers care enough to wonder how it turns out.

An unclear or reactive protagonist: Confusing or slow-to-start beginnings can be the result of an unclear or reactive protagonist. Look for multiple points of view with characters all acting, but no one person, or one problem, is standing out as the main problem of the novel. Since it's not clear what the point is, or who has the problem, readers can't tell what they're reading or who they're reading about. And since no one is actively doing anything, no hero emerges.

REVISION RED FLAG: If your beginning doesn't "end" until the middle of the novel (from a page count perspective), that's a good indication that there's too much unrelated information in the front of the novel. Maybe there's excess backstory, or scenes that don't move the plot, or even too many of the same kinds of scenes that aren't serving the story. Conversely, if your beginning ends right away, that could indicate there's not enough setup and the story is starting too fast.

To fix a beginning, you sometimes need to look at (and write) the ending. Once you see how the story ends up, it's clearer where and how it needs to start.

Step Four: Fix Problems With the Middle

Most of the plot happens in the middle as the protagonist tries and fails to resolve the story problem, while the antagonist makes those tasks harder and harder. For more in-depth discussions on these issues, see Fixing Common Problems With the Middle on page 85.

Common middle problems include:

Boggy middle syndrome: Since the middle is half the novel, it's common for plots to drag and wander without direction. There aren't enough goals to drive the plot to the climax. A boggy middle is often solved by adding a major turning point in the middle of the book (the midpoint reversal). Boggy middle syndrome creates most of the problems found in middles.

Repetitive scenes: Too many similar scenes can bloat a boggy middle as you try to fill up all that space—such as, multiple chase scenes, several attempts to solve the same problem, repeated interactions between characters, and way too many conversations around a kitchen table. Repetitive scenes can indicate a middle that's light on plot, or one that needs to vary how the protagonist accomplishes the goals so the scenes are different.

If your middle is suffering from this problem, consider doing the exercises in If You Want to Develop the Scenes: Revision Option: Making Similar Scenes Feel Different on page 146.

Unnecessary subplots: Subplots often bloom as you flesh out a middle by sending the characters running around, killing time. It might add words, but it's not adding any value. For more on fixing subplots, do the exercises in If You Want to Deepen the Plot: Developing the Subplots on page 129.

No payoffs: In an effort to pile on the problems, sometimes you forget to reward both the characters and the readers for sticking with the plot. Constant failure can make a plot feel as if it's not getting anywhere, but a few victories (even if they're small), can make the plot feel like it's moving toward the end.

No surprises: You set up the beginning, you know the ending, and the middle is all about getting there. But it unfolds exactly as readers expect without any surprises, twists, or discoveries, so readers start skimming to find out how the story ends. Add in a little unpredictability and make readers want to stick around.

Dumping on readers: Now that readers are hooked, you dump all the backstory you held back from the beginning into the middle. You explain, you flashback, you infodump—and the pace slows to a crawl. If you think your middle is dumping a lot, consider doing the exercises in *Book Three: Fixing Your Setting and Description Problems*: If You Want to Eliminate Unnecessary Infodumps on page 67.

Stagnant stakes: Bad things happen all through the middle, but the stakes never escalate. The protagonist faces exactly the same danger by the end of the middle as she did when she started it. If you're concerned the stakes in your middle aren't escalating, consider doing the exercises in If You Wanted to Deepen the Plot: Developing Conflicts and Stakes on page 116.

No character arc movement: The protagonist solves problem after problem, but nothing is learned by it, and she's making the same mistakes she made at the beginning of the novel. Let the protagonist learn a few lessons and suffer a few failures.

REVISION RED FLAG: A good place to start looking to fix a boggy middle is to check how your internal conflict and character arc affect your external plot arc. If these two aren't causing trouble for each other, that's a likely trouble spot.

Middles are notorious for bogging down, so if you discover you have a lot of reworking to do in yours, don't worry. It's a common problem. As you review your middle, also keep an eye out for anything new to share with your readers, or a different way of looking at the story or world.

Step Five: Fix Problems With the Ending

The ending resolves the core conflict of the novel and puts the protagonist up against the antagonist. It's the moment readers have been waiting for the entire book (no pressure), so the most common problem is not living up to that promise. For more in-depth discussions on these issues, see Fixing Common Problems With the Ending on page 134.

Common ending problems include:

The ending is too short: The story is rushing to the payoff and not letting enough tension build, trying to wrap it all up too quickly. This indicates the climax might not be fleshed out enough and needs to be dramatized more—description, internalization, dialogue, etc.

The ending is too long: A too-long ending rambles on after the climax is over, or it takes too long to get there. It could also be that there's too much description or infodumping as you tie up loose ends. Liberal use of the delete key typically fixes this problem.

It doesn't resolve the core conflict: While getting the protagonist into and out of trouble, you forget what the point of the novel was and end up solving a problem in the climax that doesn't fix the problem posed at the beginning of the story—and the one the protagonist has been trying most of the book to solve. Try letting the climax solve the core conflict instead.

The ending doesn't fulfill the story promise: A close cousin to not resolving the core conflict is when a story changes somewhere in the middle and the ending isn't the promise made at the start of the novel. Maybe it started out as a political thriller and turned into a romance, or started as an adventure that turned into a story of self-reflection. The story promise made at the start is not kept. Keep the promise.

It doesn't involve the protagonist: The climax comes and goes and the protagonist isn't the one who finally defeats the antagonist and saves the day (however that unfolds in your novel). If the protagonist isn't the hero, then why have readers been following her all book? Put the protagonist back in the driver's seat and let her solve the problem.

There's no end for the character arc: The protagonist goes through all the deliciously evil things you did to her to get through the novel and by the end—she learns nothing, and is no better or worse off than when she started (this applies only to novels with character arcs). Give the protagonist a character arc and a reason to experience the plot of the novel.

Too many loose ends: Readers reach the end of the novel with way too many story questions left unanswered. It feels as though half the interesting problems were forgotten or shoved under the rug. Start tying up those loose ends early.

Not enough loose ends: On the flip side, endings that tie up every single loose end often feel too pat, as not everything needs to be explained and wrapped up with a bow. Leave a few questions unanswered or ambiguous (just not the ones readers *want* you to answer).

It's not satisfying to readers: Readers expect a payoff worth waiting for and this ending isn't it. Sometimes it's a matter of expectations, or the buildup was a promise that couldn't *be* kept. If you can't raise the ending to meet the promised payoff, maybe lower the expectations so the payoff works.

The stakes don't go up: The climax should be the highest stakes in the novel, but if nothing gets worse or costs more to win in the end it's not as satisfying. Try raising the stakes and making them more personal to the protagonist.

It comes out of the blue: Something or someone appears from nowhere and fixes whatever is wrong (*deus ex machina* endings). There's been no groundwork for it, no clues that it was possible, it just "magically" works itself out (often with little to no help from the protagonist). Let the characters solve the problem—don't swoop in and save the day.

It just stops: The climax happens and then it's over. There's no denouement, no wrap up, and it feels like the last few pages of the book were torn out. Another variation is an ending that reaches a certain point, resolves the last goal, and then ends. No climax, no big finish, it answers the story question and quietly fades away. Give readers a chance to come down after all that excitement, or give them the excitement they waited for.

The ending is often what determines how much readers like the novel, so do your best to craft a satisfying end.

Revision Option: If You Have a Major Plot Event That's Not Working

Sometimes you have a plot event you love, maybe even looked forward to writing the whole draft, but it just flat out doesn't work when the book is finished. It can be heartbreaking to cut it, but a necessary evil.

Here are some clues you might need to cut a critical event from your novel:

Your writer's instinct says so: You often know (even if you don't want to admit it) when something isn't working. This is a different feeling than those "is this working?" doubts we all get from time to time. Being unsure of a project is normal, but that keep-you-up-at-night dread that it's *just plain wrong*? Your instinct is on target. Trust yourself.

You're doing plot gymnastics to make it all work: Plot events should flow naturally from one to the next, and it should seem inevitable, not forced. Sometimes you get the best plots from trying to make two ends meets, but if you're working too hard to *force* it to work, it's probably better to cut or change it.

The reasons to arrive at that event aren't plausible: If you can ask one or two questions about the protagonist's motives and the whole scene falls apart, you're probably on shaky ground here. Same as when you answer those questions with "Because that has to happen for X to happen."

Resolving that event doesn't help the story: It *feels* like a major part of the book, but it doesn't resolve the problem the protagonist needs to fix, and it's not driving plot.

There are no real stakes for that event: You probably *have* stakes, but they're likely to be the large, yet vague "Lots of lives will be lost" type. On first glance they seem high, but your readers (and often your characters) don't care if it happens or not, because they're not invested in it. If this event can happen and nothing changes one way or the other for the main characters, you might want to take another look at your stakes here.

Fixing a Plot Event That's Not Working

Realizing there's a fundamental flaw in your plot is never fun, but if you look at it objectively, you can usually find the answer and fix the problem. Even if that's banging on the delete key in a big way.

Cut it: It'll be hard, but the story will be the better for it. Allow yourself to follow where your plot naturally leads. Save the original scene(s) in another file to make the cutting easier. You still have it, and can always add it back if you find a way to make it work.

Move it: Sometimes moving a plot event to another part of the novel fixes the problem. Perhaps that event will work better as a trigger to another plot point instead of the result of one.

Change who's in it: The same event might work better if it happens to or with different characters.

Change what triggers it: Maybe the event itself is fine, but how it comes to pass is wrong. Look for ways to have this same event happen, but through different means.

Change the outcome: If the event causes a problem down the line, try adjusting the results of resolving or dealing with the problem.

If you need more in-depth work on the beginning, middle, or ending, continue on to the next sessions. If these are working, skip ahead.

Fixing Common Problems With the Beginning

For these exercises, the beginning means the first 25 percent (roughly) of the novel. It's the setup and the introduction of the problem and everything that happens to get the protagonist into the main plot path and to the middle of the book.

Revision Option: If You Think You're Starting in the Wrong Place

Plenty of first drafts start in the wrong place, so don't worry if yours is one of them, or if it's taking you a few drafts to find the right opening. It's common to not know the right opening until you've written the ending.

Step One: Examine the Opening Scene

Analyze your current opening, which will be either the first scene or the first chapter if it's only one scene:

Describe how the story opens in the first few pages: Does it start with description, internalization, action, etc? What's the first thing readers see? Try to sum up your opening in one or two sentences and capture the essence of what it's doing.

Describe the goal in the opening scene: What's the protagonist in this scene trying to do? Even if the scene has nothing to do with your core conflict, the protagonist should be trying to achieve something.

Describe the conflict: Goals don't mean a lot if there's nothing in the way of getting them, so who or what is keeping the protagonist from what she wants to do? What type of conflict is creating the tension in this scene that will hook readers and draw them into the story?

Describe the stakes: What risk is the protagonist facing? No matter how small the goal, there should be a consequence for failing that will keep readers interested. If the protagonist isn't the one at risk, who else might be?

Describe in one paragraph or less what happens next in the scene: How does this opening move the plot forward? A short description will force you to look at what's going on in that scene and help you pinpoint the goal-conflict-stakes structure.

Describe how the first scene or chapter ends: This event transitions into the next scene or chapter, and is the "oh, no!" moment that will either hook readers or not. How did the previous events in the scene get readers to this moment? Where will the plot go from here? Is there a reason for them to turn the page?

Step Two: Connect the Beginning to the End

Next, step back and look at the story as a whole to see how this opening connects to the rest of the book, especially the ending:

What's the core conflict of the novel? The beginning is all about getting the protagonist started on the journey to the end. Consider both the internal and external conflicts, as the opening scene might focus on the character arc first (internal conflict) and introduce the external conflict in a few chapters.

When is the protagonist brought into this core conflict? It can be small, and it can be something the protagonist doesn't even know connects to a bigger issue yet, but there's a moment where if the protagonist turned left instead of right, she never would have had this thing (the inciting event) happen to her. That moment is when she makes a choice or acts in a way that sets her on the plot path. This is the bridge moment that connects the opening to the rest of the novel (if the opening scene isn't the inciting event itself).

What's happening when the protagonist triggers that moment and steps onto the plot path? Stories typically start in the normal world of the protagonist's life, so the protagonist will likely be doing something normal that doesn't go as it usually does. What is she doing when this plot path moment occurs?

How does this event connect to the core conflict? You should be able to make a step-by-step list that shows how this event leads to the end of the novel. If you can't, that's a red flag that this isn't the inciting event, and that's likely the problem.

Is the opening the inciting event? If so, and you still think something is off, the story might be starting too early and needs more setup or a few more scenes before you reach this point. Try creating a smaller problem that introduces the protagonist and the world and *leads* to the inciting event.

If the opening does nothing to get the protagonist onto the plot path (the inciting event), or onto a path that directly leads to the inciting event, that's a strong indicator that this isn't the right opening for the novel.

If it does, then you're probably starting in the right place.

If you *are* starting in the right place, but think the opening isn't as strong as it should be, look closer at your goals, conflicts, or stakes in the scene. If those look good, move on and examine the narrative drive. Consider doing the exercises in If You Want to Strengthen the Narrative Drive on page 147 for more insights.

If the drive still feels off or weak, look back at your opening scene analysis. Is there anything you didn't answer, or half-answered (be honest)? If so, this is likely the problem. Answer those questions again with the core conflict in mind, and this time dig for the honest answers.

If this doesn't fix the problem, and everything looks good but something is *still* off, look at (and be ruthless):

The first few pages: What is the protagonist doing on page one? Is she active or is there more description or narrative that sets the scene?

Perhaps there's too much setup and that's bogging the scene down. If you're not sure, try highlighting in different colors what lines are action, internal thought, description, backstory, and infodumps. Look at the color balance. Where is there too much? Not enough? Make the protagonist active and give her something to do that will get her to the first step of the core conflict.

The opening scene goal: Is the goal apparent from the first page, or is it a goal that appears later in the scene or chapter (or several chapters in)? Sometimes the protagonist is doing something unrelated at the start of a novel to setup the scene, and the real goal is mentioned several pages in, delaying the beginning of the story. Show the goal right from the start and make it clear what the protagonist is trying to do.

The opening scene stakes: Even if it's clear what the protagonist is doing, if readers don't care if she succeeds or not they won't be curious enough to keep reading. Are the stakes worth worrying about (again, be honest)? Even a mundane scene can have meaningful stakes if the protagonist cares enough about the outcome. For example, not buying milk when a character knows it'll cause a huge fight with the spouse does matter, even if it's just about milk. But stopping off for a latte that has no repercussions at all doesn't give readers a reason to stick around.

If the current opening scene isn't getting the protagonist to the inciting event or core conflict, look at the *next* scene and evaluate that one as a potential opening scene. Keep moving forward until you find the right opening scene, or you determine what scene puts the beginning back on track.

Revision Option: Dealing With Too Much Setup

Every beginning has setup in it, but there's a difference between good setup and bad setup.

Bad setup explains the story, typically using infodumps, flashbacks, and backstory. It stops the story because there's no goal or reason for it to be there aside from dumping information.

Good setup refers to the elements that flesh out the story and lay the groundwork for the plot. It's conveyed in a way that establishes a character, world, or situation all while moving the plot and story forward at the same time.

Step One: Eliminate Unnecessary Infodumps

If the information isn't needed to understand what's going on in that scene, and does nothing but dump in facts and explain, it doesn't need to be there and is likely bogging the beginning down.

For example, if you want to set up that being out on the street after dark is dangerous, show the protagonist being nervous about going out after dark, or have her think about it being a bad idea. Show how someone afraid to be out after dark would *behave*, and avoid a paragraph-long infodump about the *reason* it's dangerous to be out after dark and why that reason exists.

Ask, "What is the reason for this infodump?" If it's to *show* X, look for a way to show it. If it's to *explain* X, cut it and see how the scene reads without it.

If you find a lot of infodumps in your beginning, consider doing the exercises in *Book Three: Fixing Your Setting and Description Problems*: If You Want to Eliminate Unnecessary Infodumps on page 67.

Step Two: Eliminate Unnecessary Flashbacks

Look for any flashbacks added so readers will "get" an upcoming scene. Instead of flashing back, use details that will suggest how the flashback affected the character.

A good flashback is a revelation, not an explanation. A subtle difference, but it changes how readers absorb the information. If they're figuring something out, they'll read on. If they're being told what's important in the story, they'll likely start to skim to get the key plot details.

Fixing Weak Flashbacks

If you have a flashback that needs to be there, but it's weak, here are some options to strengthen it:

Flashback to events readers *want* to know: If you've teased readers with a secret for a while, and they're *dying* to know what happened, a longer flashback will usually hold their interest. Pique curiosity first, then give them the information once they crave the answers.

Make the flashback relevant to the situation: Information revealed in a flashback should advance the plot and move the story forward. It can also be something relevant to the character's development. Using a flashback to trigger a realization can be quite useful.

REVISION RED FLAG: If the flashback doesn't do these two things (it's not relevant to the scene and readers won't care about the information), there's a good chance you can cut it and insert the information another way.

Keep the flashback short: The longer readers stray from the main narrative, the higher the chance they'll start skimming to get back to the main plot.

Keep flashbacks in the character's voice: If there's a reason for a character to flash back on a memory and she remembers it in her voice, it will feel more natural.

Give longer flashbacks the same drive as a regular scene: If the flashback has its own goal-conflict-stakes structure, it will draw readers in and make them curious to see where it goes. The longer you ask them to pause the main storyline, the more responsibility you have to entertain them during that side trip.

Flashbacks can be an effective tool when used well, and they can help eliminate backstory. A few lines of memory can often dramatize a past fact a lot better than exposition, and help characterize to boot.

Step Three: Streamline the Focus on the Protagonist's Normal Life

Common writing advice says to start with the protagonist's world before you change that world. The problem comes when there's no conflict for the protagonist to encounter, so the "day in the life of" is just watching the protagonist go about her (often boring) day until something "suddenly" happens and she's dragged into the plot. In a beginning, this is deadly.

🚩 **REVISION RED FLAG:** Look for the words "suddenly," "without warning," "out of nowhere," or something similar just before a big action scene. Odds are, this is when the action starts and everything before it is bad setup you can trim back or cut entirely.

Often, you'll find backstory and infodump mixed in with the "typical day" as well, trying to add some excitement or interest to what your instincts are telling you is a boring setup scene. Trust those instincts and cut what isn't vital.

Revision Option: Not Enough Setup

Stories that start too early usually need *more* setup to ground readers in the world and introduce them to the protagonist. Too much too fast is thrown at them and they have a hard time keeping up and understanding why what's happening is important.

Step One: Add Necessary Groundwork to Set the Scene

A little groundwork goes a long way. As long as readers understand the general gist of what's happening, and they find that compelling, they'll keep reading to see what happens next. If they're lost, they'll stop trying to figure it out. Make sure:

It's clear who's in the scene: Faceless people can be hard for readers to absorb, especially if they're not sure who the protagonist is. "The man" or "she" with no hints as to who these people are can put readers at a distance and not let them connect to the story as they should. After all, if the character isn't important enough to name, why should the reader care?

It's clear where the scene takes place: Readers need to be able to picture where they are, and a sense of location allows them to ground themselves in the setting.

It's clear what's happening in the scene: Show the goal and what the protagonist is trying to do to give a sense that something is happening and the story is moving on page one. The specifics can be a little vague if you need to maintain mystery, but give readers the basic details to understand the context of what's going on. For example, you don't have to say the characters are breaking into a bank, but let readers know it's a robbery. Or, let them know the building is a bank and going in there is creating tension between the characters, but surprise them with the robbery.

It's clear why it matters: Stakes create interest and give readers a sense of where the danger lies. They can't worry about the protagonist if they don't know what she's risking.

It's clear where it's going: Setup is a lead in, so it needs to lead somewhere. If there are no hints where the plot is going, it can feel aimless and uninteresting.

Adding setup doesn't have to give secrets away or explain anything you don't want it to. Readers want the mystery and the wonder, but they also want context for it. Often, all a scene needs is a few specific words or lines to provide that context.

Revision Option: Fixing a Lack of Story Questions

Story questions can mean any number of things—a literal question a character asks, a situation that suggests a question, a mystery that makes readers and characters wonder, the meaning behind an odd detail or bit of dialogue—whatever works for the story. They're *not* the questions readers ask because of confusion about what's going on. Confusion does not equal suspense, and problems with story questions usually fall into this area.

Step One: Add Story Questions to Hook Readers

Look for places where you want readers to question or wonder something, and either add a question, or tweak what's there to nudge readers into thinking and wondering about it.

🚩 **REVISION RED FLAG:** Watch for questions posed right in the text. It's common in a first draft to state outright what you want readers to wonder about instead of maintaining a little mystery. Sometimes this is good; sometimes it bangs readers over the head and is too obvious.

Add literal questions: These are questions posed by the characters. The protagonist might say or think, "Where's Papa going with that axe?" and then readers will want to know as well. Literal questions make readers wonder the same thing as the character, then tag along to find out the answer.

It's not uncommon to see literal questions within goal statements, such as, "Did Bobby kill that boy? I had to find out." They're flashing lights that tell readers what the plot is going to focus on for a while.

🚩 **REVISION RED FLAG:** Too many literal questions can hurt the tension, so use them carefully. They work best when they're questions the character would logically ask at that moment, not a rap on the head by the author telling readers what to wonder about.

Add situational questions: These are questions created by an unusual situation that draws readers in and makes them curious about what's going on. Who are these people with guns lurking outside a school? Why is that woman agreeing to be put to death? The clues that provide the answers to these questions are missing and readers will read on to find out what this is all about.

This type of "what's going on?" is different from the confusing type, though. With a situational question, what is *happening* in the scene is clear, but the *reasons* behind it are a mystery. It's more about discovering the who or why than the what. For example, readers can see that armed men are studying a high school, but who they are, why they're studying it, and what they plan to do is uncertain.

A confusing "what's going on?" scene would show the same people planning an attack on a building, but not mention it was a school or that they had guns. The compelling parts are missing, and there's not enough context to understand what's going on at the basic level.

Add emotional reaction questions: These are questions created by emotions. Something is brewing in the story that will cause the protagonist (or another character) to react emotionally in a way readers anticipate—both negatively and positively. Dread is just as strong as hope in these types of questions (often stronger if the stakes are super personal).

If the protagonist is clearly headed toward something bad (or even good), readers will hold their breath to see what will happen and how the character will react to it. Readers might even fear that outcome, knowing what it's going to do to the character they love.

Add information questions: These questions focus on the discovery of information. Usually the type of information the protagonist is looking for is clear, and revealing that information is the goal—such as the protagonist discovers a coworker broke into her office and searched it, and she sets out to discover why. Sometimes it's more subtle with clues dropped by the author that only readers see—such as hints that suggest the protagonist doesn't know the truth about herself; perhaps she's adopted, or she has a special ability.

How something came to be is another example, and one commonly seen in genre fiction. How does a world that forces its children to fight to the death on TV happen? Why is everyone scared of an eight-year-old girl? Readers want to know how or why something is the way it is and they'll read on to find out.

Add teaser questions: These are questions posed when answers to previous questions lead to *other* questions. Readers get an answer they've been dying to know, but it only opens the door to more mysteries, more delicious reactions, more unknowns. Perhaps the protagonist finds proof Howard shot the sheriff, but readers *know* Howard was in another state at the time.

REVISION RED FLAG: Questions that drag on and *never* get answered can weaken the suspense of other questions (because why worry about something if the author has proven they won't answer it?). They also have less impact because readers don't fully remember why they wanted to know the answers in the first place.

Story questions are important, but be wary of posing too many of them at once. A flood of questions can leave readers struggling to remember details and undo all the work you put into creating those mysteries. Just like your plot and character arcs move the conflicts, a solid arc of questions that build and lead to more keeps the overall novel moving forward.

Revision Option: Fixing a Reactive Protagonist

You often wind up with a reactive protagonist when you're not sure what the protagonist wants from the novel. You know the premise, and what must be done to explore that premise, but there's no main character with a problem working within that premise.

Step One: Make the Protagonist Act to Create the Plot

The protagonist drives the plot. She makes it happen through the choices she makes and the results of those choices. Revise the beginning so that:

The protagonist makes choices that affect how the plot unfolds: Look for places where the protagonist acts only because an outside element forces her to. Find ways to make the outcome be her choice instead— even if outside elements *create* the need for that choice.

Those choices cause events that would not have happened had she not made that choice: Look at the choices the protagonist makes. Edit any outcomes where it made no difference which option she chose. Find ways to make the choice affect what happens at that moment, down the line, or even better—both.

The protagonist plans and acts out those plans to achieve a desired result: A proactive protagonist is trying to solve a problem and achieve goals. Look for places where events are happening *to* the protagonist, and find ways for her to get into that trouble by her own choices and actions.

The protagonist has goals to strive for: Find tasks for the protagonist to do. Look for places where she's just reacting to whatever is happening in front of her and adjust it so she's more in control (even if things are out of control). If everything is going crazy around the protagonist, she should still try to act, even if you know it's pointless and will do nothing to help her. It's the act of trying that matters.

The choices the protagonist makes and the actions she takes create the plot for the novel. Without those choices, the protagonist is just along for the ride.

Revision Option: Fixing an Unclear Protagonist

An unclear protagonist is most commonly found when:

The focus is on the problem: The core conflict and problem to solve in the novel aren't personally connected to any one character—so there's no personal goal to drive a protagonist and no stakes to motivate her.

The focus is on the idea: The novel is trying to explore an idea more than solve a character's problem. In premise novels, the concept is all that matters, and any old character will do as long as you can tell readers all about this cool idea.

In essence, it's when you forget you need a character to solve a problem within an idea.

To clarify who the protagonist is, look for ways to connect her to the core conflict, and give her a series of goals to solve to avoid an unpleasant consequence. If you have multiple point-of-view characters (common in these cases), one character typically stands out as the main character, even if the points of view are balanced, such as in a romance with both parties as point-of-view characters. Ask yourself:

Who is the character with the most to gain and lose? This is typically the protagonist.

Who has the ability to act and effect change? The protagonist drives the plot and creates the story.

Who must be there for the story to happen? The protagonist is the only character who must be in a novel for it to work. Even the antagonist can sometimes be a non-character, such as in a Person vs. Nature story.

An unclear protagonist is frequently a character issue, because the protagonist isn't fleshed out enough yet to be that "person with a problem." If this is the case in your manuscript, consider doing the exercises in *Book One: Fixing Your Character and Point-of-View Problems*.

If not, then focus on adding details and goals to make it clear who the protagonist is. A lack of internalization might be the problem here, so consider doing the exercises in *Book One: Fixing Your Character and Point-of-View Problems: If You Want to Streamline the Internalization* on page 107.

Beginnings can be tricky, but it helps to remember that their job is to pique your readers' curiosity, sweep them away in your story world, and prepare them for the plot ride ahead.

Fixing Common Problems With the Middle

For these exercises, the middle means the center 25 percent to 75 percent (roughly) of the novel. It's the efforts and failures of the protagonist to resolve the core conflict, and everything that happens to get the protagonist to the climax in the last 25 percent (roughly) of the novel.

Revision Option: Unclogging a Boggy Middle

Middles tend to sag because a lot of time and effort is spent setting up the story, and an equal amount of time and effort is spent on the climax and ending, but the middle gets less attention. It's like an airport terminal where the characters wander around, grab some food, and hang out until the call for the climax is heard.

Not a good recipe for a happy middle, let alone a happy ending, since readers have probably wandered off to do something else by now. Luckily, a boggy middle can be fixed by giving the protagonist problems to solve—or else.

Step One: Add a Midpoint Reversal

The midpoint reversal is a major event in the middle of the novel that provides a goal for the protagonist to work toward, thus providing narrative drive through the middle, and something exciting for readers to anticipate (or be surprised by).

A good midpoint reversal:

Reveals new information that changes how the protagonist views her world and problem: The midpoint can also work as a fake out, where the protagonist thinks she's won, but the truth is the exact opposite. The protagonist gets everything she *thought* she wanted, but it turns out that's the worst thing that ever could have happened to her. "Success" has terrible consequences she was completely unprepared for. Or "failure" is exactly what will lead her to victory in the end.

Takes the story to a new level by raising the stakes and piling on the pressure: The first half of the novel gets the protagonist into trouble (of her own making, naturally), and after this point, the trouble gets piled on (often by the antagonist) and she must reap the consequences of every mistake made so far. The midpoint is the beginning of everything about to go horribly, horribly wrong for the poor protagonist.

Starts stripping away the protagonist's support system: As the antagonist gets the upper hand and the stakes get higher, people the protagonist has relied on (and used as a crutch) are no longer there for her. Sometimes her own actions cause the problem, but it can also be because she never truly knew the extent of the problem and now she does. Characters who were willing to help no longer can, or are no longer willing to. Assets are taken away. Access to necessary resources vanishes.

Starts a ticking clock: It's not uncommon to introduce a hard deadline during the midpoint to help raise the stakes and make the situation harder on the protagonist. The full extent of the problem is often revealed here, and now the protagonist knows what's barreling toward her at high speed.

If you're stuck with a boggy middle, ask:

What is the absolute worst thing that can happen to the protagonist in the middle of the novel? Now consider what changes if this *actually happens*. How does it affect the scenes leading up to the middle? Does it give the protagonist more to do? Does it tighten the pacing since all the scenes now lead to this big event? If not, keep brainstorming ideas until you find one that offers you a solid plot path to get there and keep the middle moving.

Is there a way to make the protagonist's inner goal clash with the outer goal in a disastrous way? Midpoint reversals are excellent places to have a victory in one area (say a plot win), but a loss in another (say a character arc loss). The second half of the middle is dealing with the ramifications of that loss (or the unforeseen consequences of that win).

What's the one thing that could happen that would make the protagonist give up? Make that happen in the novel's middle, then devise a reason why she *won't* give up. The second half of the middle often has the protagonist slipping farther and farther away from her goal, driving her to the dark moment just before the climax. Finds ways to force her to that low point.

Are there any deep, dark secrets that could be revealed and ruin everything? Information that changes everything characters (and readers) thought they knew can shake up a boggy plot and get it moving again.

Can you mirror the climax? Sometimes a midpoint reversal will foreshadow what's to come, either by showing the protagonist failing or hinting at what she'll need to do to win.

The midpoint reversal is a major turning point in a novel that welds the front and back half together. Everything that came before it has led to what occurs after it, and it's all in jeopardy (which is why it's so much fun to write).

Structuring a Middle

If you're not sure of the best way to structure your middle, plan out a few turning points and build a plot foundation. You probably have three to five big plot events that happen in the middle (if not, this is a problem). One launches it, one surprises readers in the middle, and one ends it, and often you'll see two more points between the beginning and the middle, and the middle and the ending. These are usually smaller plot points or subplot moments.

It typically looks like this:

Start of Act Two problem – minor problem one – midpoint reversal problem – minor problem two – end of Act Two problem.

Start of Act Two problem: This is the problem created by trying to solve the inciting event or story catalyst from the beginning. The protagonist spends the first half of the middle trying to resolve this problem.

Minor problem one: The plan to solve the Act Two problem runs into a snag. It's common to see a subplot around this time, often connected to the character arc.

Midpoint reversal problem: A major problem is discovered, possibly sending the story in a new direction or shaking things up.

Minor problem two: A snag occurs in the plan to fix whatever problem occurred at the midpoint. Often, the midpoint changes the situation so all the protagonist's plans are useless and she has to come up with a new approach. It's also common for the antagonist to cause the reversal, and now the protagonist is struggling to stay ahead and not fail spectacularly.

End of Act Two problem: The protagonist discovers a major problem that will be the focus of Act Three, and will lead directly to the climax of the novel. This is typically the lowest point in the protagonist's arc.

The middle is all about deepening the story, allowing the beginning and the ending to come together in a way that satisfies your readers.

Revision Option: Fixing a Lack of Payoffs

In an effort to pile on the problems, sometimes you forget to reward both characters and readers for sticking with the plot. Constant failure can make a plot seem like it's not getting anywhere, but a few victories—even if they're small—can make the plot seem like it's moving toward an end. See what wins you can give your protagonist that move the plot without making the obstacles seem too easy. Maybe the wins can be from a subplot or emotional aspect to provide the payoff.

Revision Option: Adding Surprises

Middles can easily turn into a "here's how the plot unfolds" series of *how* the protagonist solves the problem, not *if* the plan will work. They become too focused on getting readers to the ending and forget that the middle is why readers picked up the book in the first place—to see what happens as the protagonist struggles to find the answers and solve the problems.

Surprises keep the monotony out of plotting, defying your readers' expectations and making them want to read every word, because they never know when something new or unexpected might appear.

Look through your middle and find the scenes where something happens in the plot. Ask:

Was it obvious this was going to happen? Some plot points *are* going to happen as expected, but there's a difference between predicable and inevitable. Inevitable feels like the hand of fate arranging situations despite how hard the protagonist tries to fight it. Predictable feels like the protagonist is following directions. Look for places where you can do the unexpected and surprise readers.

Did the protagonist do exactly what she said she would do, exactly as she planned? Often, the protagonist lays out the plan and explains everything before she starts in an attempt to establish the goals and stakes (which is good). But it goes too far and ends up sabotaging your middle, because readers now know exactly how it will play out. Look for any planning sessions and cut out everything but the bare minimum to establish the goal and get the plot moving.

Did any of the potential risks or problems occur? Just saying there *are* risks isn't enough if nothing happens, or only the risks mentioned ever occur. Look for ways the stakes and potential dangers might come to pass, but not in the way the protagonist thought. This will alert readers that something bad is brewing, but surprise them with how.

Do the characters behave as expected? Middles are good times for people to screw up, act out of character due to stress and fear, and generally break from the pressure. Look for ways to surprise readers by having a character do the last thing they'd expect.

For more on plot twists, see If You Want to Deepen the Plot: Developing Plot Twists and Twists Novels on page 132.

Revision Option: Restarting Stalled Character Arcs

Sometimes character arcs stall, because you know the protagonist needs to change, but you didn't spend enough time figuring out how. So the protagonist solves problem after problem, but nothing is learned by it, and she's making the same mistakes she made at the beginning of the novel.

REVISION RED FLAG: Check how your internal conflict and character arc affect your external plot arc. If these two aren't causing trouble for each other, that's a likely trouble spot.

A lot of first drafts stumble in the middle, so don't worry if yours needs more work. In most cases, simply adding a midpoint goal is enough to give the plot the necessary drive to ramp up from the beginning, and speed down toward the ending.

Fixing Common Problems With the Ending

For these exercises, the ending means the last 25 percent (roughly) of the novel. It's the final march to the big battle against the antagonist, where the protagonist uses all she's learned and resolves the core conflict.

Revision Option: Fixing Too-Short Endings

Too-short endings typically happen when you don't leave enough time to build up tensions before the climax. You go from Act Two to the end in one or two steps and rush the plot. In the rush, it's common to skip important elements such as description and internalization. The ending turns into a fast-paced, dialogue-heavy whirlwind, or it's one long summary of the action.

If your ending seems too short, look at your plot and consider:

How does the protagonist start her journey toward the antagonist? Common story structure dictates that right before the ending begins, the protagonist will undergo a failure or dark moment when all seems lost. It's the dark before the dawn, the moment when everything comes crashing down. The protagonist makes a decision to move forward and face the antagonist, whoever or whatever that is. The journey to the antagonist is how you create the necessary buildup of tension.

Look at how long it takes your protagonist to reach the antagonist. Odds are the path between the dark moment and the climax is pretty short (making the ending feel short), and adding a few more steps and obstacles will slow the pace down.

If the issue is too much summary, take those described moments and turn them into full-fledged scenes. Dramatize instead of summarize.

How many obstacles are thrown in the protagonist's way? One way to test this is to examine the beginning and count how many obstacles kept the protagonist from stepping onto that plot path in the first place. Beginnings and endings often mirror each other, so the paths might be similar.

Also look for any subplots that need to be resolved before the ending. These are all useful elements to add conflict and give a sense of forward momentum as the protagonist marches to the climax.

REVISION RED FLAG: Be wary about adding obstacles to delay the resolution. Too many of those can create the opposite problem (an ending that's too slow or never ends), and bog down the ending. Aim for plot complications that also reveal something interesting or new in the story, or allow the protagonist to exhibit a needed skill for the climax.

How has the protagonist changed, and what examples show that change and growth (the character arc)? The ending often shows how the protagonist has grown and developed the skills necessary to defeat the antagonist in the end. The previous obstacles overcome and problems solved all show how the protagonist has learned from her mistakes and is now (readers hope) ready to face the antagonist (or show she's still refusing to grow and this is her last chance).

In a too-short ending, this growth might have been left out or glossed over, so those last final growth moments aren't seen. The protagonist changes suddenly to be what she needs to be, but there's not enough of that growth displayed in the end to make it plausible.

Look for situations and opportunities that show this growth, and add them where needed so the protagonist is growing at the same times she's figuring out how to defeat the antagonist.

Can you add one last surprising twist that raises the stakes or reveals critical information? Another reason an ending can feel short is because it unfolds exactly as expected. The predictability makes it feel rushed (even if it isn't) because readers are waiting for something new that never comes.

Look for ways to add a surprise or have the ending unfold unexpectedly. This is when long-held secrets might be revealed as well, especially if those secrets will put the characters in the worst possible mindset for the final showdown.

Even small twists can help create unpredictability, so don't think you need a major twist to make it work. Look at each step in the protagonist's plan and think about your options. Did she choose the most obvious path, or can the plot go a slightly different (and unexpected) way? What might happen if events don't turn out as expected but still keep the plot on track?

How does the protagonist battle the antagonist? Sometimes, the final battle is over too quickly, and all your buildup evaporates in a few paragraphs. This should be the hardest battle, the toughest fight, the most difficult decision the protagonist faces in the novel. If the defeat is a breeze, it cheapens the entire story.

Look for ways to make the final battle harder, tougher, and more developed emotionally. If you're light on description, add more detail and further develop both the setting and how the action itself is conveyed. If you're light on internalization and dialogue, look for places where the protagonist can think about what's going on, toss in a quip, say something, or even talk herself through it.

How does the protagonist win (or lose)? The final moment of resolution is a major event in the story. If this goes by too fast, readers won't feel the emotional impact they need to be satisfied by the ending. If it's too easy, they'll feel cheated. While you don't want to drag this out unnecessarily, if the win is rushed, it can make the whole ending feel rushed and leave readers confused.

Look at how your protagonist wins and see if you need to add more description or internalization, or if it needs clarification of what happens.

How does the story wrap up? Some stories end right after the protagonist wins, dropping readers mid-emotion. It's jarring and can feel like someone kicked them out of a moving car. A little wrap up is a good thing, and helps ease readers down from the excitement of the climax.

Look at how you transition from final battle to last page. If it all wraps up too quickly, it might be leaving your readers behind.

Revision Option: Fixing Too-Long Endings

Too-long endings drag and make readers groan and say, "Will this ever *end*?" You want that sense of events building to a climax, but too many obstacles can make the story feel as though it'll never end because there's always "one more thing" that must be overcome or resolved.

Sometimes, too-long endings result from too many subplots or story questions that need answers before the book ends. There's too much left hanging to fit everything into the ending, so it feels bloated and overdone.

If your ending feels too long, ask:

Are there obstacles that are there only to delay the ending? With so much emphasis on creating conflict and struggle, it's easy to go a little too far and add too much.

Look for obstacles that don't change how the ending unfolds—they just slow down the time it takes to get there. Cut any that aren't critical to the climax.

Are there plot wrapups or denouement events that can come *after* the climax? Some events can wait until the final wrap up to be resolved, such as showing how so-and-so finally reached home. The fate of smaller, yet loved, characters and what happens to them can be a nice way to finish off the story.

Look for resolutions that don't need to be resolved in the climax or even the third act. Some of these resolutions might be better resolved late in Act Two if they help make tasks harder on the protagonist.

Is there an order the resolutions need to happen in? Depending on the importance of the various characters, you could pace your ending by how you arrange those characters' endings. Smaller reveals might build perfectly to the big "oh, wow!" moment.

Look at what you want to resolve in the end and determine what tasks need to go where and why. Think about how these smaller resolutions can make the climax stronger.

What priority are the resolutions? This is important if you have smaller subplots or lesser characters you're wrapping up. Their plot resolutions might come earlier in the third act, because they aren't critical to the plot. Major characters and major storylines would likely be resolved at or near the end, because that's what readers are looking for.

Look for anything that doesn't absolutely need to be there and either cut it or move it out of the ending.

Can any of the resolutions be smaller asides and not full-blown scenes? Not every character in the novel needs a fairytale ending, especially secondary characters. If a subplot can be resolved in a paragraph or two, let it.

Look for mini-endings within your ending, where the focus is on non-protagonists wrapping up their own storylines. The more time it takes to wrap those up, the more likely it is you can cut them back.

Revision Option: Fixing Endings That Don't Resolve the Core Conflict

The core conflict (the point of the book) should be tied up. That's the promise you made to your readers and they expect you to fulfill that promise. This is the reason the story exists in the first place—to solve this problem.

If the core conflict isn't resolved, that can indicate a few things:

You're not sure what the novel is about: This is a tough call to make, because it usually means there's a lot of rewriting to do to fix it (and at this stage, the last thing you probably want to do is more revision). But you can't resolve a conflict if you're not sure what that conflict is. You can't go forward until you fix that problem.

Go back and examining the beginning of the novel. Usually, the core conflict is stated somewhere in the beginning, and it's clear what must be done. Pay particular attention to the inciting event and the Act One problem. These two moments are where the protagonist enters the plot path and becomes drawn into the story proper. The rest of the plot is simply resolving the problem discovered in one (or both) of those moments.

If you realize you don't know what that core conflict is, consider returning to the plot and structure analysis sections and re-evaluating the plot (on page 53). You might also want to skip ahead to the If You Want to Deepen the Plot section on page 107 to nail down what your core conflict truly is.

In rare cases, you might need to go back to the planning stage and do some heavy brainstorming to find the conflict (I suggest picking up a copy of the first book in my series, *Plotting Your Novel: Ideas and Structure* in this instance).

You don't know what the protagonist's goal is: Depending on how complicated the story is, or how many characters there are, it's possible you lost sight of the goal and forgot what it was all about on a deeper level.

Look at your protagonist and ask what she wants and what she's been after the whole time. Somewhere in the story, the protagonist likely said what she was after and why it was important. If not, that could indicate you have a premise novel on your hands and no one is driving the story.

You might also try re-evaluating the character arc, especially if the story is more character-focused. It's possible the growth didn't happen or the ending isn't fixing that internal problem.

You changed what the novel was about somewhere along the way: Sometimes stories change, and what you thought you were writing isn't what you ended up with, so the ending you planned isn't the right ending for this new and improved story.

Move backward from your ending and determine where the shift in story occurred. An idea probably hit you at a precise moment and the protagonist changed focus and goals. What she wanted no longer applies, and you'll need to revise the beginning and/or the middle to add this new plot or direction into the existing storyline.

How extensive the shift is will determine how much rewriting is needed. A small shift might require only a few tweaks here and there to nudge events back on track, but a major shift might require major re-plotting. Re-doing your editorial map with this new direction can help ensure your story is working the way you want it before you do any additional rewriting.

You're not done yet: In some cases, what you think is the ending really isn't. Maybe it's an exciting step on the way to the climax, and it feels right because it's well-written and defeats a major villain, but it's not *quite* there yet and doesn't resolve the whole problem.

Look at your ending and see where the story can move forward to the core conflict ending. Try listing the steps needed to resolve that goal and compare it to the ending you have. What changes? What's missing? How might you combine the two aspects of the story so it all blends smoothly?

REVISION RED FLAG: If the ending *isn't* the core conflict, but you feel strongly that it's the *right* ending, that could indicate the core conflict isn't what you thought it was. Look at the problem the ending resolves, and determine if that's what the novel is about. You might have to go back and re-plot sections of the novel to lead to this resolution instead.

Revision Option: Fixing Endings That Don't Fulfill the Story Promise

Sometimes a story will *technically* resolve the core conflict, but do it in a way that doesn't keep the story promise made to readers at the start of the novel. Often, this happens when the reasons behind resolving the core conflict change, and the protagonist's motives or needs shifts. Maybe she wants to see the killer found, but what was once a story of revenge suddenly turns into a need to put that death behind her. Readers will be thrown when the protagonist forgives the killer instead of taking revenge.

Not only will broken promises cause you revision nightmares, you'll destroy the entire story in the process. Take a look at your ending:

Remember what your core conflict is: Your story is trying to solve a single problem (even if it's complex) for a single reason. There will be other factors that influence this reason, but something is motivating the protagonist to act. Make sure your protagonist resolves *that* problem for *that* reason using the skills and lessons learned over the course of the novel.

If the protagonist's motives need to change in the story, make sure there are hints and clues along the way so the change in focus isn't jarring. Don't promise a story of friendship that turns into something else by the end.

Don't let subplots hijack the real story: Subplots are shiny, they're fun, and they're often filled with emotions, but they're *not* the point of the novel. If one takes over and demands to be the star of the ending, kick it off the stage.

Readers will trust you to keep your promises and give them the story you agreed to tell them. Don't let them down.

Revision Option: Fixing Endings That Don't Involve the Protagonist

Since the protagonist is the one driving the story, and the one facing the core conflict, the ending needs to have her solving the problem.

Look at your ending and ask:

How does the ending affect the protagonist? The protagonist must be affected by the problem or she wouldn't be the protagonist (if not, that could indicate you have the wrong protagonist and might consider doing the exercises in *Book One: Fixing Your Character and Point-of-View Problems*: If You Think You Have the Wrong Protagonist on page 62).

Look at how the ending matters to the protagonist and what role she might play in it. What does she need to do to make it all come out right? What skill does she bring, or knowledge does she have that will make all the difference?

How might the *protagonist* solve the plot point of the book? Sometimes you have several characters who are all deeply connected to the core conflict, even though they're not the official protagonist. If another character is facing the antagonist and doing all the work, what happens if you let the protagonist do it instead? A simple shift in who does what at the end could fix the problem with minimal effort.

Look for ways to put the protagonist back into the plot-driving seat and make sure she acts to resolve the problem. Other characters can help, but if she wasn't there, the entire final battle would fail, or maybe not even happen.

REVISION RED FLAG: If the person resolving the core conflict and facing off against the antagonist is the only person who can do it, that could indicate *that* character is the real protagonist of the story.

Revision Option: Fixing Endings That Don't Resolve the Character Arc

In more plot-focused or series novels, the protagonist doesn't grow all that much and there's no strong character arc (so there's nothing to resolve here). But in most other novels, the protagonist learns through the experiences in the novel and becomes a different (usually better) person by the end of the story.

If there's no growth at all, that could indicate a lack of inner conflict, or that the novel's problem isn't personal enough to the protagonist. She's solving the problem because she's told to, not because she cares or has anything at stake.

It could also indicate that the growth stalled and the plot took over. The story is no longer about the protagonist figuring out X while solving Y, it's just focused on solving Y.

Look at your story and ask:

What inner conflict has your protagonist been struggling with all along? Dealing with this inner conflict typically plays a big role in the ending. Either this is the flaw that must be overcome to defeat the antagonist, or it's what's been holding the protagonist back all this time and getting in the way of her happiness.

Look at the flaws, weaknesses, and even dreams of the protagonist. What needs to improve or be fixed? How might that problem be solved by what the protagonist undergoes and faces in the climax?

Also look at how the character arc has been unfolding so far (don't forget to refer to your character arc map). Is there a moment where the growth stopped? Check any notes you made about when and where growth should happen that might have been left off or obscured.

How can you make that inner problem conflict with the outer problem in your climax? Character arcs create tension and conflict, and if the protagonist has to make serious and deep personal changes in who she is or what she believes in order to win, that final showdown will be tough.

Look for ways in which the inner conflict is hindering (or helping) the protagonist as she faces the antagonist. Where might it make the situation harder or the choices tougher?

How might that inner conflict influence what the protagonist needs to do to solve the final problem? Realizations of the "right path to take" are fairly common in a climax, as the protagonist takes that last step of the character arc and grows into who she needs to be. This is frequently a path she never would have chosen had she not undergone and faced the problems of the novel.

Look for ways in which the problems the protagonist overcame to get there can influence how she resolves the core conflict of the novel. She *uses* what she's learned.

Revision Option: Fixing Endings With Too Many Loose Ends

While you don't have to tie up every loose end in a novel, leaving too much unresolved can lead to unsatisfied readers.

Rule of thumb: The bigger a deal you made out of something, the more likely it is you'll need to tie it up in the end. If a good part of the story goes into trying to resolve a conflict, resolve it.

However, series books often have a primary conflict that spans the series with steps to the larger story arc. It's okay to leave those hanging, as you can't exactly give away the ending of book three in book one. If the goal of book one is to get to X so the protagonist can ultimately do Y in another book, it's okay to leave Y hanging in a series. The point of book one is to solve for X.

If you're not writing a series and think you have too many loose ends, consider ways to:

Identify the plot threads that need tying: Determine which threads should be tied up and which ones can be left dangling. Anything you've spent time teasing readers about will probably need to be dealt with, while smaller throwaway clues can usually stay unresolved.

Connect the threads: Look for any threads that serve the same plotline or story arc. It's possible you can resolve multiple connected questions in one scene. Also look for smaller or less important threads and see if they can be resolved earlier.

Space out the threads: Examine when and where a thread is resolved, as the resolutions affect a novel's pacing. Too much information (such as revealing what it's *really* all about) at once can leave readers confused or unable to absorb (and remember) it all. If a lot of threads need to be tied up, look for ways to space those reveals out so readers get a little bit at a time and aren't overwhelmed.

Tying up plot threads can fix a slow scene, so look for scenes and moments that could benefit from a little information boost. If there hasn't been any new information revealed for a while, it might be the perfect place to tie up that loose end.

Revision Option: Fixing Endings With Too Few Loose Ends

Readers can complain if you wrap up the plot *too* nicely. It's not realistic, because life is messy and problems don't always solve themselves in the end. If your ending is a little too pat, you might:

Untie a few ends: Look through your plot and subplot resolutions and see if any could be left unresolved without hurting the novel. Maybe it's enough to know that the two sidekick characters have feelings for each other, and readers don't need to see for sure that they get together. Or maybe that lost or missing detail remains a mystery, leaving readers to wonder about it after the novel is through.

While a few dangling ends can feel real and create some fun mystery, make sure anything vital to the story is resolved. If it's something that will hurt the resolution of the entire novel, tie it up.

Leave a few mysteries unexplained: Not everything in the story needs to be explained. If knowing how or why something works as it does has zero effect on the outcome of the plot, then perhaps leave it for readers to wonder about.

Not every character needs an ending: You love your characters and you want to show what happens to them, but the farther they are from the protagonist, the less readers will likely care. Sure, they liked reading about them, but they don't always need to know where that minor character will go now that the world is saved.

Revision Option: Fixing Endings That Don't Satisfy the Reader

A satisfying ending is subjective, so it can be hard to know if your ending is doing its job or not. You want your ending to be a surprise, yet still feel inevitable.

For some genres, the ending is obvious and inevitable and *won't* be a surprise (such as a murder mystery or romance). That ending is *why* readers picked up the novel—to see the hero win, the couple united, the child saved.

It's *how* you get there that makes all the difference.

Look at your ending and pose it as a question: For example, will Frodo get the ring to Mt. Doom? Will Bob and Jane find love? Will Nya save her sister?

This is the plot goal of the book, and it'll be a yes or no question. Readers expect the novel to answer this question. What's satisfying to readers are the events that occur between points A and Z—how the protagonist solves her problem, how it affects her, and what price she pays to do it.

If you're unsure if your ending is satisfying or not, ask:

Does it resolve the core conflict of the novel? This is the big "this is what my book is about" question that your protagonist has spent the entire novel trying to achieve.

Does it satisfy the major questions posed in the novel? You don't want to tie up *all* the loose ends, but you'll want to tie up the major issues in the story your readers will want to know the answers to.

Is this the ending most readers are hoping for? This one can waffle a bit, because we've all read books where we wanted one ending, but the book ended another way. If you do have an ending that isn't how readers will likely want it to go, make sure it's clear that that's how it *needed* to go to make whatever point you're trying to make.

What price does the protagonist pay for this resolution? Have you ever been to a sporting event where you didn't care for the sport or either team? Did you care who won, no matter how good the game was? Readers need to care about the outcome, and if the protagonist fails and loses nothing, then the problem is meaningless. Even if failure means something horrible happens to other people—if it doesn't affect the protagonist or characters readers care about, they *won't* care.

What new information is revealed that connects to this problem? Last-minute twists, final reveals to long-awaited secrets or mysteries can happen in the end to surprise readers. The discovery that things weren't what they seemed or there was more to it can add surprise to what is inevitable.

⚑ **REVISION RED FLAG**: However, withholding a key piece of information until the end—a piece that just happens to be the thing that makes everything clear and solves the problem—risks making readers feel lied to and cheated. If there's no way readers could have ever guessed the whole reason behind everything until you told them, you'll have unhappy and angry readers. Surprise them, don't trick them.

Is the ending meaningful? Happy or sad, the ending should *mean* something to satisfy readers. There should be a point to the problem and the effort it took to resolve that problem, and a reward for readers who spent X hours to read this story. Maybe the resolution is clear, maybe it's vague and ambiguous, maybe it sets up the next step in a larger story—but it *ends*.

What constitutes a satisfying ending is up to you (and the reader I suppose, but that's beyond your control). What you want to say with the ending is also your call. It's your decision what emotions and thoughts you leave readers with when they finish.

Revision Option: Fixing Endings That Don't Raise the Stakes

Some endings don't cost the protagonist anything more in the final battle. For example, her life was in danger before she started the fight, and it's still in danger as she enters the fight. There's nothing else to lose. The stakes *feel* like they've gone up, but they've only gotten bigger and more impersonal, which lowers the risks as far as readers are concerned.

Look at your ending and ask:

Are the stakes more personal or just bigger? Thousands of people suffering is bigger than the protagonist and her friends suffering, but readers don't care about thousands of faceless characters. The stakes look higher, but it doesn't matter if people readers aren't interested in are affected.

Look for ways to make the final stakes more personal to your protagonist. Let it cost more to win, and have greater rewards for that victory (and greater sacrifices for failure).

Is the only thing at stake the death of the protagonist? This is a common "stakes never increase" problem in first drafts. On page one, the protagonist's life is in danger if she doesn't resolve this problem, and by the end, her life is still in danger if she doesn't resolve this problem. It feels huge (life and death usually is), but nothing the protagonist does (or has done) has affected her fate. It's still all or nothing.

Look for ways to work up to the life-or-death consequence, or find other ways to hurt the protagonist besides loss of life.

Does nothing change? In some cases, resolving the core conflict doesn't change anything. It's hard to accomplish, sure, but the protagonist's life is no better or worse off at the end than when she started the journey back on page one. It's common to see life and death stakes here, but since that's never an option it doesn't carry any weight with readers. They know the protagonist won't die, and nothing less has any affect on her life.

This issue usually requires more work to fix, as it's typically caused by an inherent flaw in the story. Look for ways to make what's happening matter to the protagonist, and give her consequences for failure and rewards for victory. Not resolving this issue will have long-lasting effects on her life and cause her pain or suffering on some level, either physical, mental, or emotional.

If you're concerned about your stakes, you might consider doing the exercises next in, If You Want to Deepen Your Plot: Developing the Conflicts and Stakes on page 116.

Revision Option: Fixing Endings That Come Out of the Blue

A *deus ex machina* ending (endings where a larger, unseen force comes in and makes it all work out) are problematic because the author, not the protagonist, saves the day and resolves the problem. There's no way for readers to anticipate or determine what will happen, as nothing the protagonist has done has any effect on the outcome of the story. The "hand of God" reaches down and fixes the problem.

These endings usually feel contrived, often based on huge coincidences or even brand-new information appearing from nowhere. Characters develop never-hinted-at skills, someone or something the protagonist barely noticed back on page five suddenly appears and is the key to everything, the protagonist makes a leap in logic that no one would ever make—whatever it is, it's so unrealistic it makes the ending of the novel feel pointless. The journey to get there didn't mean anything, but the problem is solved by outside forces.

If you think your ending might be coming out of the blue, ask:

How is the ending resolved? Look at how the ending unfolds. Can you see specific actions the protagonist takes to get from problem to resolution? Did those actions affect what happened?

How is your protagonist involved? The protagonist should be the one who makes the ending happen through her actions. Her choices and plans led to this moment.

Could readers have anticipated or guessed this ending? Out-of-the-blue endings usually shock readers (and not in the good way), because there's no groundwork in the story to prepare for them. Key information is either too well-hidden or never shown, and the ending draws on and depends on details that appear moments before they're needed. Or worse—how it happened gets explained afterward.

Is the ending based on coincidence? A good rule of thumb for coincidences is: Coincidences that hurt the protagonist are good, but coincidences that help the protagonist are bad. If events have to work out just right, and characters just happen to be in the right spot at the right time for events to unfold as needed, then the protagonist isn't doing enough to drive the plot and resolve the ending on her own.

Does an outside force or lucky break help the protagonist win? Sometimes these events can fall right on the border of acceptable—such as a person or event that made a brief appearance earlier suddenly arrives at the right moment to help. It can *feel* okay—after all, the protagonist did help that old beggar man in chapter two—but it's so far-fetched it stretches credibility; the beggar man turns out to be the most powerful magician in all the land and decides to lend a hand because the protagonist was nice to him once.

Lucky breaks can also feel this way, though sometimes that Hail Mary pass *does* land, and that once-in-a-lifetime shot hits the mark. These can be tough, because gasp-worthy surprise victories *do* happen. The trick here is to let the protagonist do all the legwork, so that lucky shot feels like the result of hard work, not a lucky break at the right moment.

In most cases, fixing an out-of-the-blue-ending means putting the protagonist back in the driver's seat and letting her cause the ending's events to happen. Spend some extra time doing the exercises in, If You Want to Deepen Your Plot: Developing the Goals and Motivations on page 114 and the exercises in If You Want to the Develop the Scenes on page 140.

Revision Option: Fixing Endings That Just Stop

It's tempting to end the novel after the climax. You've done so much work and you're tired, and you just want it over. But novels that end when the bad guy hits the mat (so to speak) leave readers feeling as though they missed something.

Endings that simply stop are some of the easier issues to fix because they usually just need a little more to wrap the plot up. The climax is over, the core conflict resolved, and it's now time to let the characters take a breath and get on with their lives.

If your ending just stops after the climax, try showing:

The characters' reactions to the victory: The characters have been working all novel to resolve this issue, so let readers know how they feel about winning (or losing if that's the way the story ends). Give readers the emotional payoff they've been waiting for.

How the resolution changed the protagonist's life: If this victory brings about a much-needed change in the protagonist, readers will want to see that change. Look for ways to show how the protagonist is different now, and how that has made her life better (or worse) and changed who she is.

Where the protagonist and key characters go next: While you don't have to lay out the rest of the characters' lives, a hint or suggestion that they're headed in the right direction to get their hopes and dreams is enough for most readers. You can show the first kiss and hint that it will lead to happily-ever-after, or show the sun coming out on a new and brighter day without fear.

Look for ways to let readers know life goes on for the characters they've come to care for and that those lives will be the ones they hoped for all novel.

The larger or far-reaching ramifications of this victory: In some stories, the goal is to make large-scale changes in the world, and readers will want to see if those changes occurred or had any effect. Small examples that indicate the situation will get better will leave readers hopeful that everything will indeed turnout okay.

Look for ways to add clues, or even state outright where appropriate, that life has changed and the world is heading onward on a new path.

Endings often need a few tries to get right, so don't worry if you have some rewriting to do. Keep reminding yourself that the ending resolves the problem stated in the beginning.

If your story structure is now solid, move on to ways to deepen your plots and subplots.

If You Want to Deepen the Plot

There are some plot problems almost every writer runs into in almost every draft. Sometimes you need to write the first draft so you know enough about the story to be able to fix these issues, and they clean up with little trouble. Other times, they're deeper-rooted problems that take more work to fix.

In this session, the goal is to address any plotting issues discovered in your analysis.

If you get stuck, remember the cornerstones of plot: What do your characters want and what are they going to do to get it?

Step One: Fill in Any Plot Holes

A common plot hole is a scene where the characters are doing what they *need* to do for the plot to unfold, but the reasons might be weak or non-existent. Readers don't know why this event or situation is happening, or there's no explanation of how it could happen based on what's been seen so far.

To make it all seem logical, look for:

A previous event or situation that can affect the problem scene: Chances are your scene doesn't exist in a vacuum. If it does, you might want to look at the sessions on fixing episodic chapters in Step Three. Something had to happen for your characters to be at this point. Go back and look at each of the key scenes that led the protagonist in this direction:

- Where did the protagonist make a choice that would affect this scene?
- Where did something unforeseen occur that affected this scene?
- Where did the protagonist miss a clue (or where could she miss one) that would affect this scene?
- Can the antagonist cause a change through her actions?

A character who can act or choose differently to change the outcome: A simple choice can change how a situation later unfolds. This is especially true if the problem scene involves an item, or a piece of information. Having a character find or learn something early on that can simmer in readers' minds until it's relevant can set up what you need to have happen without it feeling contrived.

- Where might a character make a different choice to achieve the desired outcome for that scene?
- Where might new information be revealed that affects a decision?
- Where might information be withheld instead?

A new way to achieve the desired result: Sometimes you need to step back from the scene and look at it objectively. Forget what you wrote or planned. Consider what steps *need* to happen for this scene to work. Then look back and see where any of those steps might take place:

- Where did the plot go off track?
- Where might a clue be discovered to lead it where it needs to go?
- Where might a character do or say something to lead in this direction?
- What might be added to achieve this result?

Don't be afraid to look elsewhere for the real problem. Sometimes it's not the scene you think that's "broken," but what came *before* that scene that's causing trouble. Look at the scenes leading up to the problem and see if adding more groundwork would make the scene turn out just fine.

Step Two: Fix Contrived or Coincidental Plots

Is the protagonist *always* finding the right person at the right time, who happens to have the *exact* item she's looking for? No matter how exciting a story may be, when the plot hinges on coincidences, readers feel cheated. If solutions to problems are falling into the protagonist's lap with little to no work, the plot will feel contrived.

Plots work best when events happen for reasons rooted in character goals and motivations and not because the author wanted it to unfold that way. There's a fine line between situations that read plausibly and those that read like a series of unlikely coincidences.

Unlikely is the key here. Coincidences *do* occur in real life, and often you'll find one or two in a story. It only becomes troublesome when a high percentage of plot events rely on coincidence to make them happen, *and* they get the protagonist out of a jam.

Rework to remove any problem coincidences and give plausible reasons for events to turn out the way they do:

Make sure the protagonist causes this event to happen: Let a goal lead directly (or indirectly) to this event happening.

Let a needed plot coincidence relate to the protagonist's goal: Maybe the coincidence is a result of a choice made, or a result of a previous action. For example, the protagonist chose to ignore A to deal with B, and now A is coming back to bite her in the butt. Or she tried to fix C and that made B happen.

Make sure the other characters in the story, especially the bad guys, have a plan: Antagonists with plans and goals of their own make much better villains, because their actions have motives, and that keep their plans from seeming random. The plan is grounded in strong motivations and goals just like the protagonist's, so even when the protagonist is trying to solve one problem, the antagonist is chugging along on his own, causing trouble.

Find a plausible reason for the coincidence to happen: If two strangers both have kids attending the same school, them running into each other at a school event is plausible, even if the coincidence happens to be the right thing at the right time. But those same strangers running into each other on a random street at a random time will feel contrived. Readers don't need much to maintain believability—they *want* to buy into your story. Show events aren't *entirely* random, and they'll go with it.

If your characters are after something for a reason and their paths cross logically, you reduce your coincidence level considerably. But they also have to *work* for it. They have to uncover clues, overcome obstacles, face internal struggles, complete the tasks that make figuring out the solution plausible.

Step Three: Fix Episodic Chapters

An episodic structure often develops when you have a series of location or goal changes and you lose the thread tying the chapters together. Events are happening, possibly even exciting "doing all the right stuff" things, but information is being put out there and it's not *going* anywhere. There's no cause and effect between chapters, even if there is within scenes.

You might have an episodic plot if:

You can shift chapters around and the plot doesn't change: This is a big red flag, because it indicates the scenes are self-contained and aren't affecting what comes after them. If six chapters can happen in any order as long as it's all before the Act One climax, they're episodic.

Every chapter has a different, unrelated goal: While you want all your scenes to have a goal, if those goals aren't steps in a larger plot, they're not doing much to advance your story. Look at where those goals lead. Is the resolution of one setting up the next? Does the next chapter start with an event or decision created by the previous goal? Does it continue with that previous goal and lead somewhere new?

The early chapters are just setting up later chapters: Foreshadowing is good, but if you have a lot of chapters in a row that are there *only* to set up later events, readers will wonder what the point is. World building and backstory chapters are common culprits here. What happens in them doesn't matter because the point is to show some aspect of the character or the past that will have relevance later. The scene goal is just something to make the scene work since you *need* a goal.

How to the Plot Moving Again

Luckily, reincorporating episodic chapters isn't that tough. It usually just takes deepening the connections already under the surface, and adding a common thread that ties everything back to the plot.

Look for ways to:

Connect the goals: How might you connect the goals in these chapters so they trigger each other? Are there external events pushing your protagonist toward her decisions that can be connected? Look at the major plot event for that part of the novel—what are the steps to get there? How can you make those steps the goals?

Connect the internalization: Can your protagonist have a common train of thought that connects the chapters? Inner conflict can tie the story together if the external conflict isn't linear.

Connect the stakes: Can the chapters all be ways to avoid the same stake? Different attempts to accomplish a similar task?

Connect the conflict: Can you bring forward a conflict that these chapters set up? Maybe foreshadow a later problem or failure?

Episodic chapters can read like random scenes, but there's a reason you wrote them, so pinpointing that reason is often all it takes to fix them. Look more deeply at what's going on and pull out those connecting threads so readers can see the story building.

Step Four: Get Sidetracked Plots Back on Track

Sometimes you can get so focused on creating problems for your protagonist that you forget what they were doing in the first place.

Here are common red flags that a plot has gone off track:

All the problem does is delay what would have happened anyway: This problem exists only to *be* a problem, and doesn't do anything to advance the story. When the protagonist resolves this goal, nothing about the overall story has changed at all. For example, completing Goal B doesn't matter, because she *still* needs to complete Goal A to avoid or prevent a consequence. You most often see this in middles, but it can happen anywhere.

The resolution to the current problem won't affect the overall story much, if at all: The problem might affect the story in a large-scale "the protagonist gets caught" kind of way, but the specific actions don't change anything. These scenes are probably decent scenes, but they're dragging the pacing or feel a little flat as a whole, and making the reader's eyes glaze over.

The resolution to the problem sends the protagonist even further away from the story goal: It's good to waylay your protagonist a little, but a subplot that requires more work than the plot to solve just so the protagonist can get back on track is one you can usually lose and not hurt the story any.

You keep adding more problems to reach a key piece of information for the plot or character: Ironically, if you have strong goal-conflict-resolution skills, you're more likely to find yourself going astray in this way because you're looking for opportunities to make the situation worse. Make sure any problems added keep your plot tight, focused, and riveting.

Fixing a Sidetracked Plot

If you think your plot has veered off track, look at each scene or plotline and consider:

How is this problem hindering the protagonist's goal? In most cases, you'll be able to answer this pretty quickly. "It keeps her from the safe house." "It stops her from meeting Brad." "It puts her life at risk." But look again at those quick and easy answers. Is keeping her from the safe house something that *also* provides a solid conflict for the overall plot, or is it one more thing getting in the way of a step that *does* connect to the bigger plot? If the problem is more delay than real conflict, it could be what's sending the plot sideways.

Is this problem different from what you've already done? It's not un-usual to have the same basic scene repeated in various ways. The pro-tagonist has to sneak past a guard to get some vital piece of informa-tion. She's trapped and has to fight her way out. She gets captured by the bad guy. Sometimes these tasks *are* important and you can't help a little repetition, but if you find yourself using a lot of similar scenes or goals just to make it harder on your protagonist, you might be throwing too much at her.

What is the protagonist trying to do from a larger standpoint, and how does this smaller step fit into that? Character goals, especially larger story arc goals, don't always start and end in one scene or chap-ter. They span chapters, with multiple obstacles to slow them down. It's a good idea to look at what the protagonist is trying to do overall (like a major turning point goal) and how the smaller goal fits into that.

The plot is important, especially in genre fiction, but if the story isn't holding that plot up, it just flops around and makes people look away. Keep your story in mind, and how your plot can serve that story.

Compelling characters need something to do, and a strong plot will al-low them to show off their skills (and reveal their flaws). A solid plot is also how you illustrate your story to readers.

Let's dig in and develop character goals and motivations next.

Developing the Goals and Motivations

What the protagonist does and why she does it drives the plot. Weak goals or implausible motivations risk making your plot weak and implausible as well. The stronger the goals, and the better the reasons for trying to achieve those goals, the stronger your plot will be.

In this session, the goal is to fix any goal and motivation issues found in your analysis, and look for ways to make the characters' choices harder.

A note about goals and motivations: The focus here is on the protagonist, but this holds true for all point-of-view characters, and even the antagonist (though often those goals are off screen).

Step One: Add or Strengthen the Goals

Add any missing goals first, as they'll directly affect how the plot unfolds, then move on to strengthening the weak or unclear goals. Weak goals are often caused by a lack of motivation—the protagonist seems as though she's following a script—so you might need to focus on the motivation first in some cases.

It's also common for protagonists to have too *many* goals, and the best way to tighten the scene is to trim out the smaller, less important goals. Try moving those extra goals to scenes that need more action or forward movement.

In every scene, make sure:

It's clear what the protagonist wants: Sometimes all it takes is for someone to say it.

The goal is specific: Weak goals are often the result of a too-vague need, such as "finding love." There's nothing to physically do to achieve that, so the protagonist can't act. But "going to the park to meet people" is an actionable goal to drive the plot and eventually find love.

It's the most logical goal for the situation: Implausible goals are frequently spotted in scenes where the easiest, most obvious path is ignored by the protagonist in lieu of some convoluted plan. It's human nature to take the path of least resistance, so if you need the protagonist to work harder to win, make sure she has reasons why she can't take the easy route.

The protagonist acts in ways to achieve that goal: Weak goals sometimes happen because the protagonist says she wants X, and then doesn't try to get it. She phones in the work and then the goal magically drops into her lap—a common problem with contrived or coincidental plots.

Step Two: Add or Strengthen the Motivations

What the protagonist does moves the plot, but why she does it moves the character arc. Goals and motivations work hand in hand to propel the scene forward.

Add any missing motivators first, then move on to the weak ones.

Look at your motivations and make sure:

It's clear why the protagonist wants to do what she's doing: Often, all a scene needs is a line or two of dialogue or internalization to make that motivation clear. There's a reason for it in your head: it just didn't make it to the page on the first draft.

It's what the *protagonist* wants, not the author: Pay particular attention to any motivation that "needs to be that way for the plot to work." For example, if the protagonist is going into the abandoned house so she can stumble across the serial killer's lair, the scene is going to feel forced. There's no reason for the *character* to act, and in fact, they way she's acting is contrary to what any normal person would do in that situation. If you need her to go inside that house for the plot to work, create a plausible reason why she'd walk through that door.

Any leaps in logic or in the decision-making process are plausible: This usually happens when something specific needs to be realized or discovered at that point in the plot, and even if the protagonist hasn't done or learned enough to plausibly figure it out, she does anyway. Common feedback for this problem are comments such as, "This seems a stretch" or, "I'm not sure how she came to this conclusion."

If you have a scene with this issue, look back at previous scenes and identify where the character encountered the reasons, clues, or steps that led her to that realization point. Are they clear? Can readers logically make the same connections the protagonist did to reach the same conclusion? A common issue here is a clue that has meaning to the author, but not the readers, so they're not seeing it the same way.

The protagonist's motivations and choices realistically lead the plot where it needs to go: Protagonists who drive the plot are wonderful things, but sometimes they take over and send the story where you didn't *want* it to go. When this happens, it's not unusual for you to force the plot back on track in a way that forces the protagonist to act in a way that doesn't feel plausible. For example, the wife of a cheating husband has been going to great lengths to eradicate him from her life, but then the plot demands she gives him a second chance, and the rest of the novel depends on it. So she does, even though there's no way she'd do it based on how the story unfolded.

The right motivation can cause your protagonist to do whatever you need them to, even if it's something no sane person would *ever do*.

After your characters are acting with purpose, take a closer look at the obstacles getting in their way—conflicts and stakes.

Developing the Conflicts and Stakes

Sit in on any agent panel at a writers' conference and you're bound to hear at least one say the most common problem with manuscripts they receive is a lack of conflict and stakes. Without conflict there is no story, and without stakes, there's no reason to care about the conflict.

In this session, the goal is to make sure your conflicts are strong and your stakes are high.

Places to Look for Conflict

Conflict—both internal and external—is all around your characters. If you think your novel lacks conflict overall, or in a specific scene, try looking at these areas first:

Family: Are there any family issues that can throw a wrench in the protagonist's plan?

Friends: Can a friend oppose, disagree, or even need help when the protagonist is least able to help?

Self: Are there personal demons, fears, secrets, or other personal issues that could cause trouble?

Work: What problems or issues can come up on the job, or because of the job?

World building: What inherent problems occur in the world?

Health: Is there a medical issue that can cause recurring trouble?

Having a better sense of where the potential conflicts lie will make it easier to add and strengthen conflicts during this session.

Step One: Strengthen the External Conflicts

Conflict is an often misunderstood word. It's easy to assume it means fighting, but conflict is just two sides opposed to the same goal. It can be adversarial (bad guy wants to nuke the city, good guy wants to stop him) or friendly (sister wants to win the race, brother wants to win the race). It can be different approaches to the same goal between friends, or even conflict within the character.

Examine any weak scenes and determine if one (or more) of these options would strengthen the conflict:

Force the protagonist to make a hard choice: Look for places where the protagonist has to make a choice, and make that choice as difficult as possible. If the answer or path is easy, brainstorm ways that aren't so clear or easy.

Let the antagonist work against the protagonist: Is the antagonist causing trouble or doing something that would result in trouble in the scene? Could the antagonist meddle somehow? What if you put them or their cronies in the same room with the protagonist? What would happen? If the antagonist isn't acting for his own reasons, even when the bad guys *are* trying to stop the protagonist, it doesn't feel like their hearts are in it.

Eliminate coincidences that work to aid the protagonist instead of hindering her: Weak conflicts often appear when the plot "just needs to go that way." For example, the author knows the protagonist will escape from jail, so the scene is written as if this is a foregone conclusion. The protagonist gets a lot of lucky breaks, the bad guys get a lot of *unlucky* breaks, and even if bad luck *does* befall the characters, it turns out to be the best thing that could have happened and works in their favor.

This is usually an easy fix—revise as if the protagonist might not succeed. Think about how the other characters or obstacles in the scene would act or work if they truly *were* trying to stop the protagonist. This will force the protagonist to work harder to win and provide real problems that feel natural to the scene.

Consider what the *other* characters want: What often holds a scene back are non-point-of-view characters who know what the protagonist wants (because the author does) so they go along with it or don't try all that hard to stop it. Friends of the protagonist are on her side and support whatever she's doing and how she's doing it. Everyone is always on the same page because that's where the plot is going.

Who might want something different from the protagonist in the scene? Are there differences of opinion in how a plan is to be enacted? Are there any ethical differences that can come into play?

Put the protagonist in an emotional or ethical bind: Doing something the protagonist knows or believes is wrong can cause a lot of trouble. It hurts, it makes her feel guilty, it could cause her to overreact about something else. Look for issues that might give the protagonist a reason *not* to act as planned.

Let the protagonist balk: Not acting at the right moment can ripple problems down the line. Look for fears or flaws that might come into play and cause hesitation at the worst possible moment.

Blow the protagonist's mind: Discovering something shocking that changes the protagonist's worldview can send her into a tailspin.

Having her world turned upside down will affect her judgment, her belief system, her self-image. When everything is off kilter, *anything* can happen. What revelation might make the protagonist question or doubt what she's doing or believes in?

Let the protagonist be wrong: If the protagonist is so sure she needs to act in a certain way, she'll ignore good advice and even warning signs she's wrong. Is there anything in the scene she's wrong about? Can there be?

Let the protagonist be right: Have you ever lied to someone and they called your bluff? Protagonists can call bluffs too, and then cause worse trouble than if they just let it go. Embarrassing someone they'll later need help from will cause trouble for sure. Is there anyone hiding something the protagonist might expose, or information she can reveal at the worst time?

External conflicts help create the problems the protagonist will solve during the novel, but those obstacles aren't the only things getting in the protagonist's way.

Step Two: Strengthen the Internal Conflicts

The heart-wrenching conflicts that keep readers glued to the pages are more often than not the internal conflicts. You don't know what a character might do when faced with an impossible choice, but you can see that choice is going to have a strong consequence.

Look for ways to force your protagonist to do what she *doesn't* want to do:

Make the protagonist go against her morals or belief system: Sometimes you have to do the wrong thing for the right reason, and those can be the toughest acts to reconcile.

Force the protagonist to make a choice she doesn't want to make: Deep down, you usually know what you have to do, even if you don't want to do it. Are there any choices the protagonist has been dreading?

Force the protagonist to make a bad choice: Mistakes are strong fodder for plot. Protagonists can mess up, and their actions cause more trouble than they were trying to prevent in the first place. This works even better if they make the wrong choice because they're trying to avoid violating one of their belief systems.

Make the protagonist fail: This one can be dangerous, so be wary of putting the characters in situations that stop the story, but sometimes failing is an unexpected and compelling path to take. It's not a setback, it's real failure with real consequences. If those consequences play off an inner conflict, so much the better.

Make the protagonist do something she'll regret: This works well if what the protagonist does early on affects the plot later. For example, a choice she makes trying to avoid one problem directly makes her obstacles tougher to overcome down the road. Maybe she can see this coming and has no choice but to do it anyway. Maybe she has no clue what problems she's about to bring down on herself, but the *readers* do.

It's easy to throw more "stuff" in the way of the protagonist, but also look at your scenes and see what mental obstacles you can toss onto the path. That can not only help deepen your plot, but deepen your characterization and themes as well.

If you struggle with conflict in your novel, try reading my book, *Understanding Conflict (And What It Really Means)*.

Revision Option: Ways Characters Can Screw Up Their Decisions

As a good person, you want to make the right choice, so it's only natural that those choices come to you first as you write. But doing the right thing doesn't always cause wonderful conflict (though when it does it's writing gold). Characters shouldn't act like people who've had three weeks to consider their options because the author took that long to write the scene. A decision made in the heat of the moment isn't the same as one made with weeks to consider.

Here are some ways your protagonist can make the wrong choice next time she's faced with an all-important decision:

Let the protagonist be impulsive: This is a helpful flaw for protagonists who need to learn patience, or who don't always consider how their actions affect others. For example, they might make snap judgments, quick decisions, or charge full-speed ahead without thinking beyond the now. If you need to get your protagonist in over her head fast, consider this mistake.

Let the protagonist make decisions under pressure: A ticking clock is a reliable way to raise stakes and increase tension in a story. Small pressures build to big explosions, so if you need your protagonist to blow her top, try looking for small ways to eat at her leading up to that explosion.

Let the protagonist over-analyze everything: If the protagonist is so busy deciding what the right thing to do is, she might totally miss the opportunity to act at all. Lost chances that lead to regrets make wonderful seeds to plant early on in a story, and can cause huge emotional trauma during that Dark Moment of the Soul at the end of Act Two. Over-analyzing can also work to sneak in possible dangers and outcomes, helping to raise tensions and keep the plot unpredictable.

Let the protagonist assume she knows it all: Perfect for the protagonist who needs to learn a valuable lesson about working with others. Let her be convinced she's always right, doesn't need advice from anyone else, and has no problem stating that fact to anyone who will listen. The fall here when reality strikes will be devastating, and all the more satisfying.

Don't let the protagonist consider all the options: An informed protagonist is a boring protagonist. Choices made without the benefit of a solid foundation of knowledge can lead to a myriad of delightful screw-ups. Maybe there's no time for research, or there's something she doesn't want to think about (denial, much?). Missing key information can send a character into a mess of her own making.

Don't let the protagonist ask for advice: Who needs a long-winded story from some old geezer about how he did it when he was younger? Times change, and what worked then surely won't work now. This is a flaw for the protagonist who doesn't respect tradition or the consul of others. The more people she pisses off, the fewer there will be when she needs them at the climax.

Don't let the protagonist make alternative plans: Plan B is overrated. An overconfident protagonist might never see the need for backup plans, because everything is going to go as she expects. So when the plan starts falling to pieces, she's incapable of wise action to correct her mistake, which causes events to snowball, getting her into more and more delicious trouble.

Making smart choices is vital in the real world, but making conflict-creating *bad* choices is a must for the fictional world. While you don't want your characters to be stupid (unless it's by design), mistakes lead to growth, and a good character grows by the end of the tale. This is especially useful for weak character arcs that need a little help.

⚑ **REVISION RED FLAG:** It's a fine line between likable characters who make mistakes and too-stupid-to-live characters who make the same mistakes and never learn. Make sure you don't accidentally turn a character into an unlikable screw-up who annoys or angers readers.

Revision Option: Ways to Make the Decisions Harder

You know what your protagonist wants, and you know why she wants it. Now, make it as hard as possible to get it.

Mix the external challenges with the internal ones: Look for ways to play the internal and external conflicts against each other. This works well because the outcomes aren't obvious, so it keeps readers guessing what will happen.

Put the character between a rock and hard place: Force characters to make impossible choices—neither option is good, but they have to do *something*.

Give each option risks or consequences: Stakes grab readers, so look for ways in which the choice has consequences and ramifications after that decision is made. Give all the options downsides—even if the protagonist doesn't see them.

Demand a sacrifice: Give the decision a cost and make it harder for the protagonist to win. Early on in a story, she probably won't be willing to make that sacrifice, but later, she'll have little choice. Offering the same sacrifice at the beginning and end of a story can be an effective technique as well. What is she willing to give up now that she wasn't before, and why?

Let the action mirror something critical that will come later: Just like a sacrifice, if there's a theme or aspect of character growth that needs to occur, try starting the groundwork for it early. If the protagonist is faced with a similar choice later, perhaps show her making the *wrong* choice early to show growth (or foreshadow failure) for that later moment.

Exploit a fear, flaw, or weakness: Is there anything the character is afraid of that you can take advantage of? Maybe it's a flaw you can show in action so readers can see how that character overcomes that flaw (and probably wins despite it).

REVISION RED FLAG: Be careful not to mistake a tough choice with one that looks tough, but really isn't. Look at the options. If the "right" choice is obvious, even though that choice is something that will be hard to do (or hard to deal with), it isn't really a choice. It's just something hard the protagonist has to do.

Revision Option: Adding Quiet Conflicts

Smaller moments can add conflict and tension to a scene without turning it into a melodramatic mess. They're great for character-driven novels where the focus is more internal than external, but also good for internal goals and character arcs.

If you have scene with weak conflicts, you might add:

Conflicts over emotions: Some conflicts are out of love. The protagonist wants to go to a party, but her best friend wasn't invited. If she goes, it'll hurt her friend's feelings. Sparing (or hurting) someone's feelings might have huge repercussions later on. Since these conflicts are personal, the stakes are naturally higher even if the conflict is mundane. No one wants to hurt someone they care about.

Conflicts over friendships: Rivalries and friendly competitions can cause conflicts, especially if they start out friendly then turn more serious. Even a constant one-upmanship can still be fun and make readers curious how the situation will turn out. Who will get the upper hand this time? Will there be a moment when that upper hand matters? They're even handy to show a skill the character might need later on without making it obvious.

Conflicts on the lighter side: Some conflicts can focus on the funny, such as a mom trying to put a diaper on a kid who's running around laughing. Their goals are in opposition (mom wants a diapered baby, baby wants to be naked and free) but there's nothing adversarial here.

While funny conflicts won't work all the time (there's often little to no stakes in this type) they can add enjoyable levity that can work well with more serious moments—a light scene right after a dark one, the calm before everything breaks loose. It can give your character something to do if the scene is mostly dialogue and feels static.

Try looking at any weak scenes to see if a quiet conflict will improve it:

- Can you make two people disagree?
- Can you make anyone else want something different from what the protagonist wants?
- Can someone try to talk the protagonist out of something? Into something? Change her mind?
- Can one person be trying to spare another's feelings?
- Can one person be trying to keep another from finding out something?
- Can someone be trapped between two others and be torn about who to side with?
- Is there a friendly rivalry?
- Does anyone want the same thing the protagonist wants? (in an "only one can get it" scenario)
- Can anyone have/get what the protagonist wanted?
- Can the conflict be played for laughs?
- Is there humor in the situation if two people disagree or have different approaches?

Step Three: Fix Low or Missing Stakes

Low stakes is the most common problem with scenes that are doing everything right, but still aren't quite working.

A handy test for low stakes is to ask these two questions:

If the protagonist walked away, what would change? This can help spot stakes that seem high, but aren't really. For example, "they could die" should be the highest stake of all, but if the protagonist walks away she'll live. Problem solved. Sure, others might die, but do readers *really* care about a faceless mass of unnamed people? Nah.

If you put the second-most important character in the protagonist's slot, what would change? Those close to the protagonist often have similar things at risk. If the story would unfold pretty much the same way, the stakes aren't personal enough. "The bad guys invade her town" is a good start, but again, so what? Anyone who lives there has that same thing at stake.

Common problems with stakes:

Stakes are too low: The consequences are either missing, or not something that would cause anyone any lasting harm. It's also common to see stakes so high they feel low because readers know they won't happen. Stakes without real bite are no stakes at all.

Stakes aren't personal enough: If the protagonist can stop at any time with no personal repercussions, why put herself at risk? Impersonal risks often indicate a lack of motivation, since there's no reason for the protagonist to act other than "plot said so."

Stakes are raised too high, too fast: Starting the stakes too high can hurt a story because tensions can't rise if the stakes can't get any higher.

Mix up the types of stakes so situations keep getting worse and worse until the end. Save the biggest risk for the climax, and build up to that. Create waves of low to high stakes, peaks and valleys like a roller coaster.

Stakes turn into melodrama: Constantly high stakes can start to feel melodramatic after a while. If *everything* is always life or death and the end of the world, then nothing matters because readers know the protagonist isn't going to die and the world won't end. Create stakes where the protagonist *can* lose.

What makes something high or low stakes is how it affects the protagonist on an emotional level. The smallest, most mundane event can be devastating to the right person in the right circumstance. The largest, most horrendous event can be just another day at the office to someone who commonly makes those choices.

Refer to your scene analysis and look for notes on low or missing stakes, or scenes where the protagonist's actions didn't affect anything, or didn't seem important enough to make readers care about the outcome.

Look for ways to:

Change or affect the protagonist's life if she fails to achieve the goal: Even if the change is small, every scene should affect the protagonist. What consequences can you add to this scene? What existing consequence can be made more dire? How might you make it impossible for the protagonist to walk away from this problem? If there *are* good stakes, can you make the risks or consequences more clear?

Have the stakes affect the protagonist personally: How might you make the stakes more personal for the protagonist? How might you narrow the focus so it affects people closest to the protagonist? How might the stakes trigger a memory or personal issue the protagonist has that makes the goal harder? How might the consequences of the action cause a personal problem?

Give the protagonist something to lose if she walks away from this problem: Failing isn't that dire a threat if there's no price to pay for it. What can the cost of failure be in the scene? What will the protagonist lose is she doesn't get the goal or fix the problem?

Escalate the stakes: If the stakes at the end of a scene match the beginning, that could indicate nothing has changed or gotten worse (stakes don't need to increase every scene, but if something's wrong with the scene and everything else checks out, this could be the reason). Where can you escalate the stakes? Where can plans go wrong? Are there any places where the protagonist wins that would be better if she lost instead?

Make the stakes clear from the beginning of the scene: Inform readers what's at stake. Sometimes it's not obvious, and the reasons behind a character's actions don't make sense. Look for places where your characters can discuss or consider the risks—even if you never plan to have them happen. It's the fear of what *could* happen that helps raise the stakes.

Just having stakes isn't enough if the stakes are minor or inconsequential. Make sure the stakes change the protagonist's life in meaningful ways.

Revision Option: Ways to Raise the Stakes

Stakes are the emotional fuel of your story and drive your protagonist to act. The more compelling your stakes, the more compelled your reader will be to see what choice your protagonist will make—and how it'll all turn out.

Look for low-stakes scenes and:

Have something go wrong: Protagonists assume their plan will unfold in a certain way, and when it doesn't go as expected, the dangers—and the risks—get higher. Look for places where mistakes can be made and plans can fail.

Make it personal: Bad things happening to faceless people don't tug at the heartstrings the same as something bad happening to someone we care about. This is why the hometown football hero who dies in a car accident hits us harder than the thousands of teens who die in car accidents every year. We know the local boy, but the others are strangers. Let the characters readers know and care about suffer.

Demand a sacrifice: Giving up something that matters a great deal shows how much is at stake for the protagonist and what she's willing to risk to succeed. Take away what matters most and force her to go get it back (or find a way to live without it).

Create cascade failure: Bad choices made early on can trigger catastrophic problems later in the story. Knowing that events might have turned out differently makes every action mean more, and seeing how the story ties together makes readers worry about even the smallest actions or choices.

Start small, get bigger: Start off with small stakes that can be escalated throughout the novel, so problems constantly get worse. Even better, look for problems that will snowball, so the small stake in the opening scene eventually turns into the dire stake at the end of the book.

Revision Option: When to Raise the Stakes

You don't need to raise the stakes every chapter, but aim for at least an escalation of stakes at major plot turning points where the protagonist is faced with a decision that will send the story in a specific direction. Moments such as:

The Inciting Event: This is usually the first time the stakes are introduced. Something goes wrong and it matters enough to the protagonist to fix it so the consequences won't affect her.

End of Act One: This is the moment when the protagonist realizes the problem isn't so little, and her first attempt to fix it failed or had unexpected consequences.

Midpoint Reversal: Often, this is the first indication that the problem affects more than just the protagonist, with glimpses of the bigger picture. Or, if the stakes have always been big picture, then this moment might be when issues become personal for the protagonist.

End of Act Two: The full scope of the problem and what it means hits the protagonist. Frequently, a sacrifice is required at this time.

End of Act Three: This is the climax, with the highest and most personal stakes of the novel. It's all or nothing, do or die. Failure is not an option.

Of course, these aren't the only places to raise the stakes. Also look for moments where:

- Choices must be made.
- Beliefs are questioned, and the protagonist must act in a way that goes against those beliefs.
- The internal conflict is at odds with the external goal. Success in one means failure in the other.
- Choices or acts are questioned, and the protagonist is second-

guessing what she's done and what it means.

Novels with strong conflicts and high stakes are hard to put down. Make the most of your scenes by tightening every conflict and raising every stake you can.

Next, let's develop how the subplots are taking advantage of all these goals, conflicts, and stakes.

Developing the Subplots

Sometimes a subplot leads you to a wonderful place you never would have found otherwise, but it can also lead you off to die alone in the woods. As long as you pay attention to the path you're on and where you're going, you'll be better equipped to tell the difference.

In this session, the goal is to cut unnecessary subplots, develop any weak subplots so they're working as intended to enhance the story, or add a subplot to flesh out the story.

Step One: Cut Unnecessary Subplots

If you did the subplot analysis in Analyze the Plots and Subplots, you should have already identified subplots that aren't working. Start by eliminating those.

Don't forget to track down any information, characters, or details associated with this subplot in other areas of the manuscript. It's common to find revision smudge—leftover bits of story—after cutting a large chunk of the novel. Searching for names or unique words associated with the subplot can help find any leftovers.

Step Two: Strengthen Weak Subplots

Subplots enhance the story by deepening something in the plot, theme, character, character arc or other aspect of the novel. Look at any weak subplots and pinpoint how and where they connect to one of these elements. These are also good things to consider if you want to add subplot.

Look at the existing subplot and consider what the focus of the subplot is:

To show an aspect of the protagonist: Subplots focusing on the protagonist typically allow her to display skills needed for the core conflict, teach her a lesson that will be needed later, give her greater understanding of herself or what she faces, etc. They're commonly connected to the character arc, helping the protagonist grow into the person she needs to be, while at the same time making her quest for the core conflict harder to accomplish.

- What about the protagonist will this subplot explore?
- Is this aspect something readers are going to want to know?
- How does this aspect aid the protagonist in the core conflict or character arc?

To show an aspect of the core conflict or story: Subplots focusing on the core conflict typically make the main story problem harder, provide avenues toward solving that problem, show a larger connection to the world, etc. They're often more plot-focused than character-focused, adding complexity to the main storyline.

- What about the story problem will this subplot enhance?
- Will it shed additional light on what it all means?
- Does it add dramatic irony to raise tensions or up the stakes?
- Does it send the protagonist toward a discovery she couldn't otherwise make?

To show an aspect of the theme: Subplots focusing on the theme are often also strongly connected to another aspect, using the theme to give greater meaning to that aspect. It might show why the fight is so vital, or what larger concepts the fight represents. It could show how the fight will affect the protagonist or what she's risking by trying to resolve the issues. Overall, a theme-focused subplot usually makes the novel deeper and richer on some level.

- What about the theme resonates in the subplot?
- How does the theme affect the other aspects of the story, such as plot and character?
- Will it create a greater understanding of the story as a whole?
- Does it shed light on the protagonist or another major character?

If a subplot isn't enhancing some aspect of the novel, odds are the story doesn't need it.

Revision Option: Evaluating the Benefits of a Subplot

Occasionally, you'll have a subplot that works as a subplot should, but you're not sure if it's doing all that much for the novel. This is especially true for novels you want to trim. It works, you like it, but is it *vital*?

Look at the subplot and consider:

Does the subplot use an existing character, or a new one? Subplots with new characters are likely less connected to the rest of the novel, so they're good candidates for deletion. They can also indicate a story tangent that's on the edge of the main story.

Does the subplot make the story better? Better can be subjective, so be ruthless here. Would the novel as a whole be worse off if you cut this subplot? What exactly does having it gain you? If it's not adding multiple layers of benefit, it might be worth getting rid of.

Evaluate the time spent vs. story gained: If a subplot only needs a few scenes to unfold, and it adds good value to the story, it's probably worth keeping. But if it requires a lot of page time for not a lot of gain, it's a good subplot to cut or cut down.

How many steps are needed to complete the subplot? Some subplots are so large they're almost novels by themselves. Is this a subplot that's close to taking over the focus of the novel? It could indicate a problem—especially if you wind up with two major conflicts to resolve by the end.

Revision Option: Ways to Add Subplots

If you think your plot is a little light and needs a subplot to enrich it, start by examining common places for subplots to flourish. Perhaps you can:

Explore a relationship: Look at the protagonist's relationships and what issues these characters deal with over the course of the novel. Consider how the relationships might change the protagonist or situation and ripple through the novel. For example, what happens if the protagonist has a fight with a jealous classmate right before she must make the hardest decision of her life? That's bound to affect her decision—and might even cause her to make a bad one.

Explore a character: Look at both the protagonist and the other major characters. Are there juicy conflicts brewing? Don't just look at conflict between them and the protagonist, but other characters and other people in the story as well. These might make excellent subplots, so see if they also develop or benefit some other aspect of the character or plot. Maybe there's a lesson to be learned in a subplot surrounding the best friend, or maybe how the love interest deals with something is a beautiful mirror for the theme.

Illustrate a theme: Look for characters who can represent your theme or a facet of that theme. What problems do they face? What are they trying to do in the novel that can touch your protagonist? Who might be a good candidate to foreshadow a choice or consequence the protagonist will face later?

Give a secondary character a small plot arc: Think about how the other characters in the novel might affect the outcome of the main plotline. Does anyone influence the protagonist at a key moment? Are there choices made that would have turned out differently if this character had not been involved? Is there an important element you want to explore but suspect it's not strong enough to be a subplot?

When developing subplots, don't forget the "arc" part of the story arc. Three points make an arc, so you'll want to have a beginning, middle, and ending for your subplot. It can have more than three scenes of course, but an arc is something readers can follow and anticipate.

If you want to add a few surprises, a plot twist might be what the scene needs instead. Let's look at those next.

Developing Plot Twists and Twist Novels

There's no formula for devising a compelling plot twist, because every plot is different and any number of things can work in a novel. But one trick for twisting a plot is pretty simple: Defy reader expectations.

In this session, examine any plot twists and make sure they're grounded in the story and not appearing out of the blue, and look for a good place to add a twist if you think you need one.

Step One: Fix Weak Plot Twists

The trick to a good plot twist is to give readers what they expect, but not in the way they expect it. Twists work when they shock readers, but then they realize they should have known all along. It's a surprise, but it feels inevitable once the secret is out.

If you think your twist is looking a little murky you might want to (and don't worry if you're not sure how to fix the issue yet—you'll explore that further in the Revision Options):

Pinpoint the clues leading up to the twist: Identify where and when clues to the plot twist are dropped. Make sure they feel natural to the scene and aren't telegraphing something to come.

Add or cut clues as needed: If you think you need more (or fewer) clues, add and cut as necessary. Look for places where the clue would most likely slide right by readers, but still linger in their subconscious.

Determine the right spot for readers to start suspecting the truth: Sometimes you'll want the twist to be a huge surprise; other times you'll want the anticipation of trying to figure it out to help pull your story along.

Determine the right spot for the characters to start figuring it out: Readers often spot details long before characters, but if it's *too* obvious, then your characters look dumb if they haven't figured it out yet. Make sure you have a good balance between reader hints and character hints.

Use twist clues to fix any slow or weak scenes: Weak scenes in need of help could be opportunities to foreshadow the twist. Would adding a layer of mystery to a slow scene help it?

Let characters encounter things thematically or metaphorically linked to the twist: Sometimes someone says something and makes you think of something different. Your brain picks up on it because there's some link between the two details that combine in just the right way. Let the characters hear or experience the perfect trigger for a memory or realization in a later scene.

A twist doesn't have to be a full-blown mind blower to work. Sometimes, smaller, more frequent twists can keep a plot unpredictable and compelling.

Revision Option: Ways to Add a Plot Twist

If you think a plot twist will fix a problem scene, look at your plot and pinpoint the obvious outcomes—even if they're exciting and wonderful and do what a good plot should do.

Once you have some candidates:

Brainstorm for the unexpected: What is the most obvious thing to do in that scene? Scrap that idea. Now what's the *least* likely thing to happen? Most times, you can scrap that idea, too, because it's so far off in left field it won't work for the book. But it usually loosens your brain enough that you start thinking about ideas that *are* unexpected, but not so far off.

Don't think about practicality at this point. When something grabs you, test how it fits into your scene and plot. Don't discard an idea because it doesn't fit or would require a lot more revision—let it simmer and see if a great twist develops from it. A twist is a surprise, and if it was an obvious fit, it wouldn't be a twist.

Reveal a secret: You can also surprise readers by revealing information that ties into the problem. You may have your protagonist resolve this issue exactly as readers expect, but then you slip in a *major* secret or detail that blows their minds and changes the meaning of the events they just saw. What they expected isn't at *all* what's really going on.

Make it worse: Ask the delightful, "What's the worst than can happen?" question on a variety of levels. What's the worst thing for the scene? For the current goal? For the protagonist's inner goal? For the protagonist's flaw or weakness? For a *secondary* character that's important to the protagonist? For the antagonist? The "worst thing" isn't always an external physical thing about to hurt the protagonist—it might be something that tears her world view apart, or shatters her beliefs, or makes her doubt something she's always trusted. It might be choosing between her, a friend, or a loved one.

Expose a liar: An unexpected betrayal can surprise readers and change expectations. So can someone who's been lying about information the protagonist thought was reliable. Or maybe the protagonist has been lying and is finally forced to fess up. Lies don't have to be for nefarious reasons either—a lie told with good intentions can be just as effective.

Let the protagonist lose: Do the unthinkable and let the protagonist lose and the antagonist win. Everything she's been fighting for is gone and now she has to regroup and find a way to go on. This is an extra sticky one though, because it can be easy to make your readers think everything they just read was pointless. Make sure that even if your protagonist loses, what she went through to get there still has meaning and wasn't a waste of your readers' time.

Ask beta readers what they think will happen, then do something else: Have your critique partners or beta readers write what they think will happen at the end of each scene and see if they guess correctly. Change as much as you can without adversely affecting your story or plot.

Revision Option: Is the Twist the Whole Book?

The problem with these types of twists is that since the reveal is secret, the protagonist usually doesn't seem to be driving the story, so the plot often reads as though the characters are wandering around aimlessly. Or worse—that the author is intentionally keeping critical plot secrets from the readers.

If you're revising a twist novel that's giving you problems, it's worth asking, "Does the plot work if readers know the twist, or is the plot all about the big reveal?"

If the novel is one long setup to, "Surprise!" there's a good chance there's not enough plot to hold a reader's attention.

The plot must stand on its own and be exciting, even if readers figure out the twist. It has to have suspense and wonder and hooks, and leave behind all those wonderful little clues that even readers who know the twist will see and delight in—and provide re-read value to go back and see what they missed.

If you're worried your novel is all about the twist, ask:

If you take out the twist, does the plot still work? Use something vague to describe the plot. For example, if the twist is that the protagonist is an alien, make it "protagonist with a big secret." If all the major plot points revolve around discovery of that secret, that's a good clue something is wrong. The protagonist should be doing what matters to her, and *in the process of that*, she discovers that big secret. Subtle difference, but it puts the narrative drive back in the protagonist's hands.

An exception here is for plots that truly are all about discovery of the secret, such as finding a killer, or uncovering a sinister plan. Readers can clearly see what's driving the plot and the effects of the secret, but the point is to work hard to uncover what it is. Uncovering the truth kinda defines those.

Is this idea to show how cool it is that you fooled the reader? This one's a toughie, and you'll have to be honest with yourself. As writers, we want to keep our readers off balance and make our stories unpredictable, but we've all read novels where the author came across as trying to pull a fast one. Key clues were held back, truths were purposely misdirected, everything was done so the author could trick the reader and by the end say "Ha ha, I so fooled you. It was X all along." If readers can't figure it out by they're paying close attention to the clues, you're not playing fair.

Are there subplots that aren't about the twist? With a well-rounded protagonist and solid goals and stakes, there will be subplots and other problems that enhance the core conflict. But if all the subplots are more ways to distract readers (or the protagonist) from the truth, then it might be a red flag the twist has taken control of the story.

Twist stories can be a lot of fun to read *and* write. Discovering the situation wasn't what you thought, and seeing the story in a new light that deepens both plot and character makes for an awesome book. But they can sometimes be a one-trick pony if you aren't careful about developing the *whole* story and are just setting up the big twist.

Finally, let's take a look at dealing with an over-plotted novel.

Fixing an Over-Plotted Novel

Often it's hard to come up with a *single* plot, but some writers can spin a tale like they have an unlimited supply. Trouble is, too many plots in the same novel can spoil a story, and knowing where the line is between complex and complicated can be hard.

In this session, prune out any unnecessary plots and refocus the novel's core story.

Common Problems for an Over-Plotted Novel

Complexity of plot varies by genre and market, and what works for a middle-grade mystery won't fly for an adult political thriller. It's a good idea to study your genre and market to see what's typical for those types of books, and develop guidelines on how much plot works for that type of story.

Common areas for over-plotting include:

Too many people: You most often see too much plot in multiple point of view novels. This structure lends itself to every point-of-view character having a story and plot of their own, and those plots often have several subplots as well.

You might be over-plotting if:

- Each point-of-view character's problem requires its own resolution.
- Each point-of-view character's problem has subplots of its own that are not connected to the core conflict.
- Each point-of-view character's problem is unique and not connected to the core conflict.
- You can't say which point-of-view character is your protagonist.

Same event, with different characters and problems: Having different characters take different elements away from an event is good, but be wary when it starts to feel like different books about a similar subject. You might be over-plotting if:

- One event creates several storylines that unfold in separate directions, while at the same time bringing nothing new to the core conflict of the novel.

- The event triggers issues or problems unrelated to each other.

- Each problem has enough meat on it to become a full book on its own.

It shows all sides, but still needs more to "get it": Adding plots to show another side or perspective because you think, "Readers won't get it if I don't," should make you pause. Your instincts are in the right place—you know you need more to make the story work—but you're looking wider, not deeper, and adding information that won't serve the story. Are you:

- Focusing only on the premise aspect of the story and ignoring the characters and their problems?

- Adding characters whose sole job it is to get one point across?

- Getting caught up in cool backstory for one (or more) of your secondary characters or antagonist and thinking they deserve their own character arc?

- Trying to tell everyone's stories?

- Pulling your protagonist in so many directions you lose the narrative drive, because it's hard to tell what the story is about anymore?

You can't easily say what the novel's about: Try writing a query letter. It doesn't have to be good, but you should be able to say in one or two paragraphs what the novel is about. If you can't, you might have too much plot going on.

- Do you need a paragraph per major character to say what the novel is about?

- Is it impossible to say what the ending is, or what constitutes a win?

- Can you pinpoint a core conflict?

- Can you pinpoint the inciting event?

- Can you write a query at all?

An over-plotted first draft isn't the end of the world, so don't worry if yours is a little bloated. Grab your editorial map and start looking for ways to trim down and get the plot back on track.

Step One: Get Your Plot Back Under Control

An over-plotted novel usually goes in too many directions, so first, decide what the story is about and what plots serve *that* story.

Ask yourself:

Who is the protagonist? This will help pinpoint who is driving the story and who has the most at stake in the problem.

What is the protagonist's problem? This will help pinpoint what the core conflict is, and allow you to cut away all the plots that don't connect to or support this.

What does the protagonist need to do to solve that problem? This will help pinpoint what aspects of the plot and subplots go with this character and this problem.

What internal struggle is the protagonist facing that connect to this problem or need? This will help pinpoint what the character arc is, and what aspects of the plot relate to this growth.

Who is the antagonist? This will help pinpoint where the conflict lies.

What does the antagonist want? This will help pinpoint what the antagonist's goals are, and how that might affect the protagonist and her goals.

How is that conflicting with what the protagonist wants? This will help pinpoint what the core conflict of the novel is and how these two sides interact.

What existing plots are critical to resolving the protagonist's goal? This will help pinpoint which plot elements are necessary to drive the plot.

What characters are critical? This will help pinpoint which characters to keep, and which to cut.

What's your overall theme? This will help pinpoint what scenes or story elements connect to the overall plot, and help you shape remaining elements to better fit the story.

If a plot doesn't connect to the protagonist and core conflict, save it for another book. It's fine for subplots to weave in and out, for other characters to share the spotlight a little, and for multiple events to be going on, but everything should serve the story and drive it toward the same resolution. That resolution may mean something different for every character, but each one will still work within the framework of that story.

Over-plotting usually occurs when you lose sight of what the story is about—a person with a problem. Put the attention back on that person trying to solve that problem and you'll find your way.

Now that the plot is all worked out, let's take a closer look at the individual scenes.

If You Want to Develop the Scenes

Scenes are the pieces that make up the plot. They connect like stepping stones, getting the protagonist from the opening scene to the final scene of the novel. From a structural standpoint, they help you focus the plot and manipulate your readers' emotions. Strong scenes make for strong plots, and thus a strong novel.

In this session, the goal is to fix any scene issues found in your analysis, and strengthen any weak scenes.

Step One: Fix Scenes That Aren't Working

Most times, if a scene isn't working it's because there's no personal goal or stakes driving it. Things are happening *to* the protagonist, not *because of* the protagonist, and she's just along for the ride.

If you have a scene that's not working, first:

Check that you have a proactive protagonist: Make sure the protagonist is actively trying to do something to solve the big story problem.

Then, look for ways to:

Clarify the goal of the scene: Pinpoint what's driving the scene and where the scene needs to go to advance the plot. You might have both external and internal goals here as well, so check to see if those goals support each other or if they conflict (both can work depending on the scene).

Clarify the conflict of the scene: What's the conflict in this scene? Something or someone should be keeping the protagonist from the goal, and it must be circumvented, overcome, or endured. What can you do to add conflict back into the scene? Who or what can be between the protagonist and her goal?

Clarify the stakes of the scene: If the stakes aren't going up even though things are going wrong, that's a red flag that it's just extra trouble and not a real plot obstacle. How can this problem make the risk higher? Personal risks to the protagonist are usually best, but you can also make problems worse for other characters important to the protagonist. Look at internal and external goals, and think about how they will affect the conflict and story down the line as well as the immediate problem in that scene.

Clarify how vital this scene is to the plot: Is this a key moment or one more tiny step in the plot? Steps are good, but too many can send the story off track if the steps aren't advancing the plot. You might have a goal driving the scene, but achieving it doesn't matter to the bigger story, so the scene flounders. If nothing will change if you took the scene out, you probably don't need the scene (or you need to make it matter).

Clarify any reveals in the scene: While not every scene has to have a gasp-worthy, plot-centric reveal, a discovery of some kind is a good way to maintain momentum. It can be new information about the world, a discovery about a character, or a clue that hasn't been solved yet.

Clarify the hand-off in the scene: Maybe the scene is working fine, but it's not doing anything to move the plot to the *next* scene. Look at the results of the protagonist's or point-of-view character's actions. Why will readers want to read the next scene, and what is the likely goal for the next scene?

🚩 **REVISION RED FLAG:** If the attempt to accomplish a goal doesn't have a consequence or trigger a reaction, that indicates the scene might be part of a series of events happening with no narrative drive. Episodic scenes often lack conflict, because there's nothing in them that moves the plot forward. Protagonist does X...and stops, then she does Y...and stops. Add a conflict or obstacle and force the protagonist to make a decision, or reveal information that will give the next scene its goal.

Is the Scene *Still* Not Working?

Sometimes, no matter what you do, a scene doesn't want to work and play well with the rest of the novel. Look at the words you use to *describe* the scene (trust me on this). You might be inadvertently focusing on the wrong narrative aspects and that's leading you astray.

How are you describing the scene? Pay attention to the verbs you use in your summary. Are your characters running, chasing, searching, crying (all active, external verbs), or are they thinking, pondering, considering, debating (all internal verbs)? If your verbs all mean "being inside a character's head," nothing is physically happening in the scene to move the plot. Revise to get the characters out of their heads and into action regarding whatever internal thing is going on.

What will readers learn or discover in this scene? Pay attention to the types of details discovered in your summary. Are they all traits or information about the character and her past, or information that moves the plot forward? If the discoveries are heavy in the character area, that could indicate there's too much backstory, infodumping, or exposition.

Aim for a mixture of discoveries, with character traits, potential problems, and plot elements. There's no perfect mix here, but try to add at least one plot detail to help move the story forward. Add in other details depending on the type of scene it is: a character-developing scene, a plot-moving scene, a set-up-scene, etc. Revise your discoveries as needed.

What will readers worry or wonder about in this scene? Pay attention to how specific the details are in your summary. Vague responses suggest vague conflict or stakes, which can make the scene feel like it's not going anywhere. If there's nothing for readers to worry about, that could indicate low or missing stakes and consequences facing the protagonist. There's a good chance there's no dangling carrot (a story question) to entice readers to keep reading. Raise the conflict and/or stakes or leave the outcome more uncertain to keep the tension high.

This will probably be one of the harder questions to answer, because a lack of conflict is a common problem in early drafts. Often, there *is* nothing to worry about because you (as the author) know the protagonist gets through the scene unscathed. Try letting the protagonist's uncertainty shine through, and making it *look* like things could go wrong, even if you know they won't.

What will make readers want to read the *next* scene? Pay attention to the story questions left unanswered and the consequences of actions taken in the scene. Vague responses here can indicate there's not enough mystery to keep readers hooked.

Also consider predictable outcomes vs. unpredictable ones. "To see if the protagonist makes it out of the hotel alive" probably won't entice readers read on, as the protagonist isn't likely to die. But "To see if the protagonist makes it out of the hotel with the information that will get her inside the secret lab" creates a scene-moving element that also advances the plot. Will she get the information? That answer *could* be no, so readers will want to read on and find out what happens.

REVISION RED FLAG: If you think you *have* to keep a scene even though everything says you should cut it, then odds are there's something about that scene that matters to the story and can't be moved to any other place. This scene is a good candidate to combine with another weak scene.

Step Two: Cut Scenes That Aren't Working

One of the harder things to do during revisions is to cut a well-loved scene, but not every scene is right for every plot.

If you're not sure if you *should* cut the scene, try pinpointing *why* this scene would be missed. Often, there's something in there that you don't want to give up.

Make a list of everything that has to stay and consider why you want it there. Is it because:

It lets you keep a well-written line you love: You'll probably have to cut the scene. Many a writer has forced an entire scene just to get one kick-ass line in there. You know those movies and TV shows where there's a big buildup to a joke, and you think, "Wow, they worked hard for that one." And then the joke isn't nearly as funny as all the work it took to get there. This is the writer's equivalent. If the single line will work elsewhere, move it, but don't force an entire scene into the novel for one good line.

It lets you show a bit of cool history or motivation: You might be able to keep the information if the information can be moved. Look for scenes with similar context. If the history is about your protagonist's childhood, where else does she think about children or growing up? If it's a bad memory, are there any scenes where remembering this would make it harder for her to deal with what's happening? For motivation, where else is she acting based on this same motivation? Are there any spots that could be deepened if this bit was the motivating factor?

It lets you show something that was once important: You can probably cut it. Ideas change as you write and remnants of those ideas can linger. Maybe you had an idea you explored for a while, but a better idea occurred to you three chapters later and you built the rest of the plot on it. Can this idea be woven into something else? Are there any other places where this idea would deepen the conflict or stakes? And the hard one: Is this an idea you like, but which no longer fits the story?

It lets you show description or world building: If that's *all* it does, cut it, or find another scene to add those details in. Does the description evoke a mood you can use to enhance another scene? Is there a perfect spot where the world-building information can be illustrated and not explained?

Some items might need tweaking to fit elsewhere and that's okay, but often, getting it *out* of the story makes you realize you don't need it at all.

Revision Option: Combining Scenes

If you find yourself with several scenes with aspects you want to keep, try merging them into another scene. Look for:

Events with similar stakes: Multiple things going wrong at once can make for some gripping scenes, and allow you to layer the plot and add depth through inner conflict. One external problem might work well with an internal problem and turn a so-so scene into a *wow* scene.

Events that can be made harder if you combine them: Find scenes with similar goals, or scenes that happen around the same time that might work together. Maybe the goal of one scene will cause more trouble or increase the difficulty of another if you introduce that second problem at the same time. For example, the protagonist finds out her husband cheated on her during a scene when she has to give a career-making speech.

Ways to raise the tension in each act: From a more macro-level approach, find story arcs that can be deepened if you combine scenes in that act. Give your protagonist more choices, and make the choices themselves tougher. If both choices have consequences and outcomes, what happens if the protagonist *has* to pick one over the other? What changes?

Places where you can deepen the emotional conflicts: For the micro-level approach, find situations that tweak the emotions, not just the external goal-focused plots. If the protagonist faces an internal struggle in scene A, and an external struggle in scene B, what happens if she faces both at the same time?

Places where you can raise the personal stakes: Bad things happening can be exciting, but it's the personal that gets readers. Find scenes that are big and exciting, yet impersonal, and determine how you might add a personal moment to them from elsewhere in the novel. For example, maybe one of those, "I need this but I'm worried it's a boring scene" types. Themes can be helpful here, as a larger-than-life moment can mirror or symbolize a deeper internal issue.

Don't mix scenes willy-nilly. You want them to work together and build toward a strong plot.

Revision Option: Making Similar Scenes Seem Different

Books often have scenes common to that genre in the plot. If it's a pulse-racing thriller, it'll have lots of action or chase scenes. Romance will have lots of relationship scenes. Mysteries show lots of sleuths looking for clues. After a while, these similar scenes seem repetitive and even predictable.

If you have a lot of chase scenes where the protagonist is never caught, readers might assume she won't be and stop worrying. If you have lovers who *almost* kiss over and over—they won't be the only ones frustrated. But these core scenes are central to these novels, and are even expected by readers.

Here are some ways to make similar scenes seem different:

Change the focus: Look at any similar scenes and determine what the main focus is for each one. How might you shift that focus to achieve the same story goal, but make the scene different? Can any of the scenes end with the current goal being the *result* of something else happening? Can a larger issue drag the characters away from what they were focused on? Can a smaller annoyance become the main problem and the main problem shift to a smaller annoyance?

Change the goal: The core conflict should tie into everything, but if every scene is "let's save the girl!" then the novel can seem stagnant—they're *always* trying to save the girl. Maybe in one scene, show why saving the girl matters, or make it the result of a previous plan gone wrong. Maybe the goal is indirectly tied to saving the girl, but connects more to a subplot. If the goals are always about "getting something," then maybe have a scene that deals with losing it, or keeping it.

Change the stakes: If every stake is death or capture, the tension levels drop right to the floor. Look for problems or decisions that can have consequences and create stakes. Think of them as lynchpins—they might seem small at first glance, but pull one and the entire plan comes crashing down.

Also look for ways to narrow the stakes to an immediate problem or action. If "losing the guy" is the risk, maybe have the scene be something that would *lead* to losing that guy. On its own it's not a horrible consequence, but under the right conditions—catastrophic.

Change the location: Are there too many scenes around a table? In a car? In someone's room? Kick the characters out! A setting change can add all kinds of different (and unexpected) layers to a scene by working thematically with it, or contrasting it. It can add extra dangers, extra problems, and the unexpected. Think outside the box and look at places that—at first glance—look like the worst places for that type of scene to happen.

Change the emotion: Horror might be about the fear, but if the characters are *always* scared, there's nothing to contrast it against. Look at the most emotionally redundant scenes. What would happen if you used the opposite emotion instead? If the protagonist is happy, make her miserable. Terrified? Make her amused or angry. What unexpected emotions might you play with and how might that change the scene?

Change the mood: Think about how movies use mood. Someone breaking into a house in a thriller feels dark and foreboding, but a cat burglar sneaking in to steal a priceless jewel can be sexy and playful. A heist is almost always fun if the thieves are the good guys, yet sinister if they're the bad guys.

Some plots need to have similar situations in multiple scenes, but the scenes don't all have to feel the same. Mix it up and even the same scene done three times can offer something new.

Getting the scenes in order and flowing smoothly from one to the next will go a long way toward creating a strong narrative drive.

Let's tighten that up next.

If You Want to Strengthen the Narrative Drive

Narrative drive is the engine that keeps the story and plot moving forward, giving the novel the momentum it needs to keep readers hooked.

In this session, the goal is to address any narrative drive issues discovered during the analysis.

Step One: Ensure the Protagonist is Driving the Plot

The most common narrative drive problem is a reactive protagonist who does nothing to drive the plot.

Make sure your protagonist is making the plot happen (you should have already fixed any goal issues in Developing Goals and Motivations, but if not, review that next). She has an opinion on what's going on, ideas for what to do, and thoughts that might even go against what others are saying. She should effect change by her choices, and act to accomplish a goal instead of watching it come to fruition.

Your protagonist might not be in the driver's seat in a first draft (it can happen as you work out the story), but by the final draft, she needs both hands tight on the wheel. Make sure she's advancing the plot and character arc so readers always know whose story it is and why that story matters.

REVISION RED FLAG: Be wary if other characters talk more than the protagonist. A protagonist along for the ride often comes across as an observer while other characters talk, plan or even act. Long stretches of dialogue go by where she barely says a word or has a thought. There's no internalization to show how she feels about what's being said, so you could effectively yank her from the scene and readers wouldn't notice she was gone.

Step Two: Identify What Changes in the Scene

Scenes move the plot forward through goals and conflicts. Trying to achieve a goal causes action, and action causes change, so if nothing changes, that's a good indication that the scene lacks the drive to keep the plot moving.

While not every aspect of a scene needs to change every time, if nothing does, the scene is probably missing something important, or it's not needed and is a good candidate to cut.

Examine any stalled scenes and ask:

What changes in the goal? Changes in the goal alter the plot and either push the protagonist farther away from it, or move her closer to it. If the goal changes completely, there's a good chance it also changed the conflict, stakes, or both.

What changes in the conflict? Changes in the conflict are often the result of discovering new information (such as, who is *really* after the protagonist) or changing settings. As tension comes from conflict, this is an area where changes can have a major impact on the narrative drive.

What changes in the stakes? Changes in the stakes usually mean the problem became more personal. It's common to see a reveal or discovery around the same time.

What changes in the motivations? Changes in motivations often come after major setbacks or shocking reveals. Characters who start out with good intentions might sink into more selfish wants as the scene unfolds. The good guy might get sick of always playing by the rules and decide to cut loose, or the character with ambiguous allegiances might finally pick a side.

What changes in the plot? Changes in the plot are typically on a macro level, as the protagonist tries to accomplish the goal in a variety of ways. For example, three chase scenes in a row with the same resolution will feel repetitious and make the story feel stagnant, but three chase scenes with different resolutions that change what the protagonist does, learns, and feels are compelling even if they're similar.

What changes in the setting? Changes in the setting often accompany goal or plot changes, as characters move to a new location to put the plan into action.

It's worth looking at each of these potential changes to see if a change would strengthen the scene. It can also help to consider the point of the scene, both from the author's standpoint (what you want to show by having this scene there) and the character's standpoint (how she sees the scene and what she wants from it). If the point is to explain something, odds are there's not enough change going on to drive it.

Revision Option: Kickstarting Stalled Scenes

If you have a stalled scene, it's usually a lack of one of the core, scene-driving aspects—the goal, conflict, or stakes.

Review the scene and ask:

Are there plausible and strong motivations for the protagonist to be doing what the plot requires? If not, look for ways to motivate the protagonist. This might require going back a few scenes, but somewhere you probably lost the reason the protagonist is on this story path in the first place. At some point, solving the plot problem stopped being the most important thing in her life. More than likely it's because the stakes vanished.

Did the stakes decrease or disappear? When the protagonist stops caring it's usually because there's no longer anything at stake if she fails. Maybe the big bad is still out there, but there's nothing at risk for her *right now*. She feels safe, even if she's still technically in trouble or on the run. Look for ways to put the protagonist back in danger.

REVISION RED FLAG: Don't just throw random danger at the protagonist. That's equally boring because the danger doesn't matter. Look for places where failure matters to the character, character arc, or the plot.

Did the scene lose its conflict? If the protagonist is merely going through the steps to get from point A to point B, and nothing is in the way (as in, something working to prevent her from obtaining what she wants) the scene can feel lifeless and stall. Look at the internal and external goals and issues. How might you crash those two together so they're at odds with one another? Maybe have your characters disagree over what needs to be done, or have the only way to succeed require a sacrifice the protagonist isn't willing to make. Find ways to make the protagonist face a tough *choice* instead of a tough situation everyone knows she'll get through.

Has a subplot taken over? Sometimes a subplot becomes more interesting and leads the protagonist off on a wild tangent. Then it reaches a point where you don't know what to do or where to go, but you can't get the plot back on track. Look for where you left the plot highway. It might be a plot event or you might have changed the goal or motivation of your protagonist. Did she suddenly change her mind about what she wanted or why she wanted it? Sometimes an exciting subplot idea can push aside the core conflict and you'll find your protagonist has shifted goals with no strong reason to do so.

If a stalled scene won't re-start, that could indicate it's not needed. Consider how cutting it affects the novel. If it won't change anything (or change so little that it's easy to adjust), it might be best to shove it to the curb.

Another way to strengthen the narrative drive is to increase the tension and hooks, so let's explore those next.

If You Want to Increase the Tension and Develop the Hooks

The hook catches your readers' attention and the tension makes them anticipate the outcome. If readers have nothing to anticipate (good or bad), the scene feels weak and slow. That's the key with hooks and tension—it's all about the *reader*, not the character. The protagonist might have no idea a problem is barreling down on her, but if readers can see it coming, and they know it's going to affect the protagonist in a way they worry about, then the tension will be high and they'll stay hooked in the story.

In this session, the goal is to increase any low tension and sharpen any dull hooks.

Step One: Raise the General Tension

Tension is vital to your story, but let's face it—you don't always have it in every scene. A lot of first draft scenes lack tension because the focus is often on the story, the setting, or the characters (or any combination of those). Check out your scenes and:

Eliminate moments where the characters are relaxed: Any time the characters relax, that signals readers there's nothing to worry about. If no other indicators of a potential problem exist, that could result in a lack of tension in the scene. If the scene focuses on relaxing or reflecting characters, try slipping in ways to make them nervous or anxious.

On a scene-by-scene basis try adding:

Something for readers to anticipate (good or bad): It doesn't have to be big to work. A small suggestion that something isn't right can work just as well as a large declaration of plot.

Something for readers to worry about: Conflicts can come into play here. Perhaps drop hints that something will go wrong, or show that situations are not what they seem.

A bit of foreshadowing to an upcoming problem: Show that the characters are headed toward doom. This also works if they're headed toward something positive (like the first kiss in a romance).

A hint of a possible problem, even if it doesn't happen: Problems don't have to come true to be tense. It's the feeling that any second, something might come out of nowhere and surprise them that keeps readers invested.

A ticking clock: The problem that can be solved "whenever" isn't as dire as the one that needs to be solved in the next two hours or else. Even better—if the protagonist is rushing, she'll likely make mistakes, which allows you to craft tougher obstacles and cause her more trouble. Create a nasty consequence for missing a deadline. Raise the stakes. Put that "or else" in there so there's a price for failing.

It doesn't take much to raise the tension in small ways, and it adds a lot of drive to the narrative.

Step Two: Add Tension Between Characters

After you've done a general tension touch up, look at the characters in your scene. If everyone is working as one, you could be missing out on potential areas for tension.

Can anyone be actively trying to prevent the protagonist from getting or doing what she wants? Look for people with reasons not to help the protagonist. A clerk who isn't being helpful. A guard she has to sneak past. A minion of the antagonist with a full-on plan to stop her.

Can anyone disagree with the protagonist? Even if two people want the same thing, they might have different ideas on how to get it. Look for characters who might have other ideas about what the protagonist is doing. Maybe they think she's wrong, or they agree but think she's going about it the wrong way. These opposite opinions can make readers wonder if the protagonist's view is right or not, adding more uncertainty.

Can anyone have an agenda that interferes with the protagonist's plan? If two guys are after the same girl, one might try to sabotage the other. Or maybe a secondary character thinks she's protecting the hero by making sure he fails. Even good intentions can create trouble.

Can anyone be keeping secrets from the protagonist? Secrets add uncertainty and keep readers guessing, especially if they suspect that secret could affect the protagonist or her plan. Even something minor that does little more than embarrass a character if revealed could keep things interesting.

Unpredictability increases not only the tension of the scene, but strengthens the characters as well by turning them into three-dimensional people with wants, needs, and views all their own.

Step Three: Add Tension With the Setting

Life doesn't always play along. It rains when you want to go on a picnic, the restaurant that was supposed to be romantic has a busload of rowdy school kids on a field trip, or the power goes out when you need that computer. Murphy's Law happens, and the environment you put your characters into could add some conflict and raise the tension in that scene.

Can weather be a factor? Someone who's cold and miserable might say things she ordinarily wouldn't. A trip that might be easy in clear weather could be dangerous in bad weather.

Will changing location make the goals harder? Sneaking through a park you grew up next to feels different than sneaking through an area you've never seen before. A new location can add a layer of uncertainty and make the protagonist second guess herself.

Is there a setting or location that causes the protagonist stress or discomfort? If the protagonist is terrified of heights, forcing her into the air will affect how she'll act.

Don't underestimate the value of the right setting to raise the tension. Do the unexpected to keep readers off balance and guessing.

Step Four: Add Internal Tension

Sometimes a problem isn't caused by external forces, but by the protagonist's internal conflict. A personal struggle can be even more powerful because it's so emotional. Making readers wonder what a character might do in a rough situation is a surefire way to keep tensions high.

Can the protagonist face a moral dilemma? Maybe she can get what she needs, but she doesn't approve of what she'll have to do. Or she must make a personal sacrifice and she's not prepared or ready to do so. Maybe the cost of that action has far-reaching consequences. Do the ends *really* justify the means?

Can the *right* choice require going against personal beliefs? What if the "right" course of action is clearly, absolutely in conflict with everything the protagonist knows is right and true, such as doing a bad thing for a good cause?

Can the protagonist face something that forces her to address an issue she's been avoiding? This is a good tension builder for that protagonist who needs to learn a lesson and grow. People don't always want to face their demons, but if they're forced to, the fallout can be devastating.

Can the protagonist face an impossible choice? Impossible choices have no clear answer, which means readers won't see the answer coming. Maybe the only way to save the child is to let the mother die. Or something horrible will happen no matter what the protagonist does. If you get your readers thinking, "I have no idea how this is going to turn out," you'll keep them hooked.

Small changes can effect big results, so look for ways to build tension on a smaller scale, with simple changes to a character's dialogue, or reaction. You *can* raise the tension without changing how a scene unfolds.

Step Five: Add Hooks and Discoveries

Keeping readers hooked is about making them want answers to their story questions. What happens next? What else will these characters do? How will they get out of this? What's the deal with X? Why is Y doing that? Learning new information keeps readers interested and wanting to know more.

If you added reveals and discoveries to your editorial map, start there and look for any holes or weak areas that would benefit from additional hooks or discoveries. Try to:

Leave an unanswered question in every scene: What is left hanging in the scene? What don't the characters know that will hook readers and give them a reason to move on to the next scene or chapter?

Space out the plot-related reveals: Check to see if the plot reveals are nicely spaced throughout the entire novel and not all clumped together. Your major plot turning points will help ensure they're spaced to help keep the story moving.

Add backstory and character-related reveals: Is there something new to learn about the characters over the course of the novel? Look to see where and when character secrets are discovered. Aim for a mix of characters actively working to discover secrets, exhibiting a trait, or suggesting a secret.

Add world-building-related reveals: Setting and world building often fade as the novel unfolds, so look for places to keep adding new aspects of the world to show what it's like to live there.

New information creates momentum, even when the plot hits a slow spot.

Step Six: Use Secrets to Add Tension

People don't tell each other everything, and even best friends hold information back. Sometimes that information is important; other times it's just embarrassing. It's common in an early draft to have characters be a little *too* forthcoming as you work out the details, but once the story is solid, see who might not be so eager to share what they know.

In every scene, ask:

What doesn't the protagonist know? The simple act of asking this can get you thinking about possibilities. What backstories or potential complications could the secondary characters be hiding? What basic, totally predictable events in the scene can be changed to add a surprise that might deepen the plot? What character arcs for secondary characters might be created if the protagonist learns something unexpected during something mundane? What might happen that would cause a reader to say, "Wow, I never saw that coming!"

What secrets are the characters keeping? This could change how they act or how they'd influence others to act. If someone avoids a certain topic, both readers and the other characters might wonder why.

What don't the characters *want* the other characters to know? This could suggest secrets to reveal that change the scene and surprise readers, and a once-simple act could have huge consequences. For example, if the protagonist goes into his girlfriend's backpack and finds something she said she'd lost, readers suddenly wonder why she lied and what the protagonist is going to do about it.

Revision Option: Making Information-Heavy Scenes Tense

We've all written scenes where we have to convey a lot of information and there's no action to keep tension high. You can't just flop the information out there and get away with it—you have to convey all that information and *still* keep the scene tense.

Even in a scene that has no action, there are plenty of places you can tweak to keep it interesting. Consider:

How the information affects the goals: The protagonist is either telling the information or hearing it. If she's telling it, it's for a reason. What is that reason? It should be more than just "it needs to be conveyed to the reader now."

Is there a way you can make the information or the reason for telling it now adversely affect the scene goals? Is there a chance the person hearing it won't like it, or won't do what the protagonist needs them to do? Is there anything about the scene that can cause the protagonist to fail at their goal if they reveal that information now? If they're the one hearing the information, does that information affect their goal? Does it make it harder?

Think about why the information is being revealed now instead of later, and what that gains you from a storytelling perspective.

How the information affects the stakes: Something is at stake in the scene, and if that information can raise those stakes, so much the better. Even if it just adds a new layer, risk, or consequence, that's still a win. Is the protagonist risking anything by hearing or telling this information? Are the people in the scene at odds with each other over anything? Does the information raise the stakes at all? If it doesn't, can it?

If the information being revealed doesn't change the situation at all, that could indicate it's infodump or backstory you might not need.

How the information affects the conflict: If it helps solve the problem, then you might look for something to counterbalance that so there's tension again. For example, the protagonist gets the information she needs, and then has to act on it and that will cause trouble. How does this information cause trouble for the protagonist? Does the information affect her personal relationships? Does it change what she thought she knew and cause inner conflict or turmoil?

The conflict can be big or small, as long as it makes *something* a little tougher now.

How the information affects the setting: Sometimes the information *is* just details that have to be conveyed. If so, perhaps look for ways to put the characters in a "dangerous" setting when they have this conversation. Can they be in a place that has inherent conflict even if the characters themselves aren't in conflict? Could something interrupt them so they don't hear the information they need? Could it be a bad time to have this conversation, but there's no other time to do it?

If there's absolutely no tension in the information itself, then look for external factors to keep the scene tense.

How the information affects the dialogue: Even information shared between friends and allies can be tense if those friends are at odds over what to do with the information. If everyone is on the same page, try looking for ways to have them disagree. Does the other person *want* to hear or tell this information? If the protagonist is trying to get someone else to talk, is there a chance she won't be able to draw out that information? Maybe the protagonist has the information and she's trying hard *not* to talk? Is she *afraid* to talk?

REVISION RED FLAG: Check how much people are saying when they speak—short back-and-forth sentences, or long, heavy paragraphs? Speeches often indicate infodumps through dialogue, and are prime suspects for sapping tension.

How the information affects the internalization: How a character reacts to what she's hearing or saying goes a long way to getting readers to feel the same thing. Consider how the internalization can help the scene. Where is the protagonist emotionally when she hears this information? Is she worried about the information? How? Can any of her fears come true in that scene? Can something *worse* than she feared occur? What does she expect to happen? How can you thwart those expectations?

A character who's tense will make readers tense, even if there's no "action" going on in the scene. If she's worried about what she's about to find out, and she's thinking about what it all means, readers will feel it along with her.

Information-heavy scenes don't have to kill the tension if you look for ways to add excitement (even if that excitement is quiet terror or subtle longing). Layer in conflict and emotion and you'll build the tension so the characters—and readers—never get a chance to relax.

You've done a lot of plot work this workshop, so let's shift gears and take a closer look at your pacing.

Workshop Three: Pacing Work

The Goal of This Workshop: To examine your manuscript's pacing and adjust as needed to create a well-paced novel.

What We'll Discuss in This Workshop: Determining the right pacing for your novel, smoothing transition between scenes and chapters, developing strong hook lines and foreshadowing, and tightening the narrative focus.

Welcome to Workshop Three: Pacing Work

A well-paced novel means something different to everyone, and much of it depends on the genre and type of story. Readers expect thrillers to be fast paced, literary novels to have a slower pace, and everything in between to be paced fast enough to keep the story moving and slow enough for them to absorb that story.

In general, pacing works like an ever-growing wave. It rises, then slacks off, then rises again, but it rarely drops as low as the previous wave (similar to stakes). The pacing increases as it nears the end of the story, with the climax being the most fast-paced section of the novel. The speed of that pacing is relevant to the novel, so a high-octane thriller will have a different definition of fast for the climax than a bittersweet character journey of self-discovery.

Pacing is the speed at which information is conveyed to readers to achieve the best impact. There's no one ideal pacing—it varies by novel and genre—and using typically fast-paced techniques (like short sentences and lots of dialogue) can bore readers if what's going on in those sentences doesn't make them want to read on, while slow-paced techniques (description and exposition) can be riveting if readers are dying to know what happens in those scenes.

Chapter length is also a factor. One novel might use long chapters with multiple scene breaks to pull readers through the story, while another novel might use short chapters that flow together seamlessly to achieve the same goal. If the pace works, don't feel the need to comply with arbitrary structures. Keep the reader turning the pages, however it works for you.

Analyze the Pacing

If the pacing of your novel is off, it can derail the entire story. A slow start never draws readers in; a too-fast ending rushes past the payoff and leaves readers feeling unsatisfied. No matter what speed you aim for, you want that steady wave that gets faster and faster as you near the end.

In this session, the goal is to examine your pacing to ensure it's moving at the right speed for your novel.

Missing or weak hook lines, a lack of foreshadowing, too much telegraphing, or a loose narrative focus can also affect the pacing, and you'll look at those in more detail next.

Determine if the Pace is Working

Grab your editorial map and look at the pacing as a whole:

▶ **What's the common pace for your genre?** Is your pace consistent with that genre? For example, a slow-paced thriller could indicate a problem (or suggest it's more of a suspense novel).

▶ **Is it well paced overall?** Slow or fast, a well-paced novel keeps the story moving from start to finish. Look for a good rise and fall in the pacing to pull readers through the novel.

▶ **Does it grab you, does it hold your attention, do you want to read on?** Look for any slow spots or scenes that are weak but you aren't sure why.

▶ **Does something change in every scene?** If nothing changes in the scene, odds are there's nothing new being revealed to keep the story and plot moving forward. Look for what's different about the characters or situation at the end of a scene compared to the beginning.

▶ **Does the pace speed up during major plot moments?** Aim for a rush and urge to read faster as you close in on the critical plot moments of the novel.

▶ **Are there waves of fast and slow pacing throughout the novel?** Tense plot moments will typically be faster paced, while emotional or reflective moments tend to slow down. Aim for a mix of both.

▶ **Are there any spots that read too fast and readers might have trouble absorbing the information?** Check the big action moments or reveals. In the excitement to write these scenes, it's not uncommon to rush through them.

▶ **Are there any slow spots that might lose readers?** Check the transitions or reflective scenes, as these are common slow-down areas. Also look at scenes where characters catch each other up on information.

▶ **Are there any spots that encourage readers to skim?** Check any scenes that introduce details, such as a setting, a new character, or a world-building detail. When the description starts to get heavy, it often bogs down the pace.

▶ **Does every scene have an emotional hook?** Check for an emotional reason why readers want to know what happens in that scene. What will evoke an emotion in them?

▶ **Does every scene have a mental hook?** Check for a plot or informational reason readers will want to keep reading. What puzzle or mystery is being offered?

🚩 **REVISION RED FLAG:** If the pace doesn't vary much and maintains a predictable and even march forward, that could indicate not enough high (or low) points in the story.

Problems Found?

If you find any pacing issues, spend some time doing the exercises in If You Want to Adjust the Pacing on page 170.

Analyze the Transitions

How you move from scene to scene and chapter to chapter leads readers though your novel. The smoother those transitions are, the easier it is to draw readers in, while jarring jumps, awkward shifts, and missing information can all knock a reader right out of the story.

In this session, the goal is to examine your transitions and how your plot moves from scene to scene.

In the next sessions, you'll look more closely at your hook lines, examine the foreshadowing, and check on the narrative focus.

Determine if the Scene and Chapter Transitions Are Working

Any time you break a scene, you give readers an opportunity to set the novel down, since scene breaks are natural stopping points. You might even want to *create* good stopping points, such as having a character go to bed or set off on a trip, something that tells readers, "Yeah, we'll pick it up here tomorrow, 'kay?" But without something to entice readers to read on, why *would* they come back tomorrow?

Scene breaks are typically softer than chapter breaks, relying on the building sense of doom to carry readers forward. A decision has been made, the stakes have been stated, and now it's time to see how it works out. Chances are, you've have nice tension building, so start out the next scene in a way that builds on that tension and keeps it going.

Look at the final few paragraphs of every scene (and the first few of the next scene) and ask:

▶ **Does every chapter end with something that compels readers to turn the page?** It might be a cliffhanger, a secret revealed, the revelation that there *is* a secret, a foreboding piece of dialogue or image, a major decision, etc.

▶ **Is there a sense of anticipation about what will happen next?** Both the characters and the readers should feel that something is brewing, and they must keep going forward.

▶ **Is there a sense of where the plot or story is going?** Check that the plot and story move forward, and there's a sense of progression to keep readers intrigued.

▶ **Does the *next* chapter's opening scene satisfy reader curiosity, or does it jump ahead in time or location and flash back to deal with the previous chapter's end?** The opening of the *next* chapter is as important as a chapter's ending—probably more so since this is where you can lose readers if you don't make them happy. Check that chapter openings fulfill the promise of the chapter endings and isn't a trick to fool or mislead readers. For example, be wary of a chapter that ends with someone creeping up the stairs toward the protagonist, and the next chapter opens with the "danger" being the protagonist's husband coming home early. The tease that something bad was going to happen isn't real, so readers can feel manipulated.

▶ **In multiple points-of-view novels, did the next point-of-view character's scene start off with something equally interesting or did the pacing drop and the tension start over?** It's not uncommon in multiple point-of-view novels to break points of view and basically start over with a new character and rebuild the tension. Drop it too low, however, and by the time readers come back to the exciting chapter, you've lost all the tension you created.

▶ **Does the scene end with something to draw readers forward, or does it let the protagonist sleep, travel, or do something else that drops the tension and pacing?** Check that every scene ends with or gives a reason to turn the page.

▶ **Does the next scene start with the plot in motion or does it set up the scene to come?** Keep an eye out for any scenes that end with a character winding down, and the next scene starts with the character winding back up again. For example, a character going to sleep, followed by that same character waking up and getting dressed. These are inherently low-tension, low-interest activities.

🚩 **REVISION RED FLAG:** Checking the transitions is a good way to spot (and fix) a problem when something isn't working but you're not sure why. If it seems like all the right pieces are there (and they often are), but the scene drags, feels clunky, or isn't grabbing the attention it should, try adjusting how you transition from scene to scene. Maybe you're not giving readers a strong enough reason to stay with the story.

Problems Found?

If you find any transition issues, spend some time doing the exercises in If You Want to Smooth the Transitions on page 176.

Analyze the Hook Lines

Hook lines evoke an emotion in readers. They cause a chuckle, tug at heartstrings, instill dread, or pique curiosity. They're the reward for reading, and often the lines fans quote or cite as their favorites.

In this session, the goal is to ensure you have strong hook lines pulling readers through the story.

In the next sessions, you'll look at the foreshadowing, and check on the narrative focus.

If you found any pacing issues during your analysis, a lack of hook lines could be a reason. Look at the problem scenes first and determine if there are indeed hook lines that need strengthening, or if they're missing.

Determine if the Hook Lines Are Working

Scanning your entire manuscript for hook lines is time consuming, but hook lines are often found alone in their own paragraph for emphasis, or as the last line in a paragraph. Try looking for single lines first in a scene or chapter. If you don't find any, that could indicate a lack of hook lines, or that your hook lines are lost in the text itself. Look through your scenes and ask:

▶ **Does every page have an emotional hook line?** If you go more than a page or two without some emotional tug, that could indicate the scene won't connect with readers.

▶ **Does every page have a mental hook line?** If you go more than a page or two without something to pique curiosity, that could indicate there's not enough conflict or action.

▶ **Are there funny or poignant one-liners scattered throughout every scene?** If no personal lines evoke some kind of response from readers, that could indicate too much description or backstory.

▶ **Are there lines that make you smile as a writer on every page?** Strong hook lines often make us feel like "writers," and they're typically our favorite lines in the book. If you have no favorite lines on a page, that could indicate a weak scene that lacks reasons for readers to care what happens in it.

Aim for a balance of hook lines overall, between emotional, mental, funny, and poignant. The more layers you hit, the more likely you'll keep readers invested in the story.

⚑ **REVISION RED FLAG:** If you find a lot of hook lines in the middle of a paragraph, that could indicate the best lines are getting lost in the text. Move them to either their own line, or to the beginning or ending of a paragraph.

Problems Found?

If you find any hook line issues, spend some time doing the exercises in If You Want to Strengthen the Hook Lines on page 178.

Analyze the Foreshadowing

Foreshadowing is a powerful technique, but one that requires a deft hand to use well. There's a fine line between hints to enhance the mood and mystery of the story, and giving it all away.

In this session, the goal is to ensure your foreshadowing works, and you aren't telegraphing the reveals of your novel.

In the next session, you'll check on the narrative focus.

Determine if the Foreshadowing is Working

A lack of foreshadowing could slow the pacing, because there are no hints or clues to indicate something is amiss, and no subconscious clues simmering in a reader's mind. Clues dropped too hard might give away the details you're trying to keep a mystery until the big reveal.

Step One: Examine the Foreshadowing Details

The right foreshadowing details can raise tensions and make future surprises seem inevitable. A lack of foreshadowing can make those same surprises seem out of the blue and even a little contrived. Make sure you're foreshadowing the right events and laying the groundwork for those plot twists and turns. Ask yourself:

▶ **Are you foreshadowing the major events or reveals in the story?** A lack of foreshadowing can indicate that events happen without build up and with little impact, as there was never a chance to worry about them. If you drop a few hints first, then readers can anticipate what's coming—even if they don't know what that is.

▶ **Are there any slow or weak scenes that could benefit from adding some foreshadowing?** An event or clue with greater meaning could fix a problem scene by layering in more complexity.

▶ **What emotional scenes might benefit from a little foreshadowing a few scenes earlier?** If a character has a major breakdown or dark moment, get readers to start worrying about it earlier—even if they don't know what's wrong, they'll have an unsettling sense that *something* is coming. You can put them in the right headspace for a scene to have maximum emotional impact.

▶ **What "out of the blue shocker information" would seem inevitable with a little foreshadowing to lay the groundwork?** Major surprises can sometimes seem like they come from nowhere if there's not a single clue that it could have happened. Sometimes you want that shock, but these surprises are often more believable if subtle clues were there all along.

▶ **Are there any setup scenes that could do double duty as foreshadowing scenes?** Sometime you need to have certain events happen for later plot events to work. These scenes can be opportunities to add deeper meaning or foreshadow the future.

Problems Found?

If you find any foreshadowing issues, spend some time doing the exercises in If You Want to Strengthen the Foreshadowing and Reveals on page 180.

Step Two: Check for Any Telegraphing

While foreshadowing is good and can heighten tension and make the reader eager to know what will happen, telegraphing steals all the tension and takes the mystery out of those hints. It shines a light on the elements you're trying to be subtle about, which can kill the pacing since it all seems predictable.

Telegraphed clues often seem stuck in, because they aren't a natural part of the events or thoughts the protagonist is currently experiencing.

▶ **If you had no idea what a clue meant, would it still fit the scene?** Be wary of clues or details that only make sense after readers know the truth. The goal is to have a clue that means *more* after the truth is revealed, but still makes sense in the scene it's in.

▶ **Is the clue there *specifically* to be noticed by readers?** Be wary of details that have no reason for the protagonist to look/think/say/notice, aside from hinting that whatever she's seeing/thinking/saying/noticing means something.

▶ **If the reader picked up on this clue and figured it out right then, would it ruin the suspense?** Readers are smart. If knowing what that clue means will kill the story, don't make it so obvious. If you have any "hopefully they won't figure this out this until later" feelings, you might consider cutting that clue.

🚩 **REVISION RED FLAG:** If you're drawing attention to a detail because you want readers to remember it for later, there's a good chance you're telegraphing. Drop hints; don't point out the clues.

Problems Found?

If you find any telegraphing issues, spend some time doing the exercises in If You Want to Strengthen the Foreshadowing and Reveals on page 180.

Analyze the Narrative Focus

A strong narrative focus keeps the text flowing smoothly from one idea to the next, and prevents the story from wandering off and making readers wonder what the point is. Losing your narrative focus is a sure way to knock the pacing out of whack.

In this session, the goal is to tighten the narrative focus and ensure that the story is leading readers exactly where you want them to go.

Determine if the Narrative Focus is Working

Confusion often results from a lack of narrative focus, pulling readers in different directions so it's never clear what the point of a scene is.

Step One: Examine the Narrative Focus

The larger, macro focus issues should have been taken care of in Workshop Two: Plot and Structure Work as you made sure your plot was advancing well and in a logical fashion (if not, or if yours still needs work, you can continue to work on that here). Those larger steps will guide you through these smaller, scene-by-scene steps.

Although there are two checks here (scenes and paragraphs), it's fine to check them both in one pass. In most cases, there's no need to edit the scene twice unless it's severely unfocused and needs the extra attention. Most scenes will need only a quick scan to ensure nothing was shoved off focus.

If you did a fairly detailed editorial map, you might be able to check the scene-level focus there instead of in the text.

Step Two: Examine the Scenes

Make sure each scene has a point and the text is supporting that point, as well as advancing the ideas behind that point. Start with the goal for the scene and ask:

▶ **Is the goal clear?** A lack of a clear goal could indicate the scene isn't unfolding toward a specific resolution, but wandering aimlessly.

▶ **Does the goal move the scene forward?** If the protagonist isn't taking steps to achieve the scene goal, then the scene will read as if it's not going anywhere and the story will drag.

▶ **Is the bulk of the scene's information supporting this goal?** Not every scene needs to be 100 percent on topic, but if you notice multiple ideas or goals all pulling the protagonist in different directions (and not in a good, conflict-inducing way), that could indicate the scene is unfocused and trying to do too much.

▶ **Does the goal lead to the next scene?** The scene should lead the protagonist (and the plot) forward. If not, that could indicate the scene is
simply dumping information, and isn't working to advance the story.

You can have multiple goals in a scene; ensure that what the scene is
trying to accomplish is moving in the same direction. If subplots inter-
twine or overlap with the main plot, aim for clear paths that show where
each plot thread is headed and how they interact.

🚩 **REVISION RED FLAG:** If you can't identify the point of the scene
and why it's there, the narrative is either out of focus, or there's no
goal. The scene is likely providing information that serves no point at
that moment.

Step Three: Examine the Paragraphs

Since this check can require reading the entire manuscript again, focus
on any scenes you flagged with pacing problems or clarity issues (as a
lack of focus can also affect the description).

Skim through the individual paragraphs to make sure they're not a col-
lection of disconnected details. During the drafting stage, it's common
to throw in details as they come to you without considering how they fit
in the existing paragraph. When this happens, the story flow looks more
like a spray and you end up with a scattered sense of what's going on.

For example, a paragraph might open with the character looking at the
room in search of a clue, then shift to talking about a world-building
detail, then end with a statement about how she's feeling. Readers will
likely be confused about what that paragraph was trying to say.

🚩 **REVISION RED FLAG:** Consider doing a paragraph-level check of
the narrative focus if you've received feedback with a high percentage of comments that question what's going on in the scene, show confusion over character actions, or say that the pacing was too slow.

Problems Found?

If you find any narrative focus issues, spend some time doing the exercises in If You Want to Tighten the Narrative Focus on page 184.

If You Want to Adjust the Pacing

Pacing problems generally come in three flavors: too slow, too fast, and inconsistent. If you think your pacing isn't keeping readers hooked, try looking at ways to adjust how your novel unfolds.

In this session, the goal is to adjust the pacing so it pulls readers through the story at the pace you want.

Step One: Fix a Pace That's Too Slow

A slow pace typically results from not enough new and interesting information being conveyed to your readers. There are no surprises or reveals, and the story drags or becomes predictable.

Here are some options for fixing a too-slow pace:

If There Are Too Many Words

While any number of issues can contribute to a slow pace, too much of "something" is frequently the culprit—long sentences, heavy exposition, speeches—any information readers have to slog through to get to the story. The more unnecessary words you add, the slower the pace will be.

Trim out heavy or repetitive description: Look for long descriptive passages, especially if the scene is supposed to be fast-paced or has a lot of action. Trim it back or spread it out to help pick up the pace.

Cut empty dialogue: Look for dialogue that adds nothing to the story, such as greetings and good-byes, and single questions used solely to keep someone talking. For example:

> "You won't believe what Bob said."
>
> "What? Tell me!"
>
> "He said…"

In this case, "What? Tell me!" can easily go.

Cut extended internalization: Look for spots where there's so much internalization that you forget what the last line of dialogue was or what the next speaker is responding to. If the dialogue and responses are supposed to sound snappy and come right after each other, don't put a lot of internalization (or anything else) between them.

Smooth clunky or overdone stage direction: Skip the obvious details that don't add value to the scene. Be especially wary of places where a character speaks, moves, speaks, moves, speaks, all in the same paragraph.

Have something change: At the core, pacing is based on revealing information to readers. If nothing changes there's nothing new, and the pace drags. Make sure something changes in every scene and readers learn new information as a result.

If Important Information is Left Out

Missing key scene-driving elements can result in a pace that drags, because there's nothing pushing the story forward.

If nothing seems too wordy, look for:

Unclear or weak goals: Most times, if a well-written scene drags there's a goal issue. The protagonist isn't proactive, she doesn't want anything, and readers watch her go about her day in some fashion. Try adding or strengthening (or stating) the goal to drive the scene and make the protagonist actively work to accomplish something.

A lack of stakes: The next biggest offender here is a lack of stakes. The protagonist *is* acting, she *has* a goal, but readers don't care if she achieves it or not. Try making the consequences of the goal matter more on a personal level. Give readers something to worry about as the scene unfolds.

A lack of conflict: If there's nothing standing in the way of the protagonist's goal, there's no mystery whether or not the protagonist will succeed. No struggle = boring, and that slows everything down to a crawl. Find ways to add or strengthen the conflict so the outcome is uncertain.

Weak character development: Sometimes the protagonist isn't "in" the scene even when she is. Readers feel detached, as if they're watching from a distance rather than experiencing the story with the character. This usually happens when there's little internalization or personal input from the protagonist or point-of-view character. She acts, but readers don't know why or why it matters so they can't connect to her and thus don't care.

If the Structure is Out of Whack

Sometimes structure is the issue, and how you break up the novel affects how it reads. The scenes themselves might work okay, but they're not unfolding in the best sequence for the strongest impact.

The problem might be with:

Bad chapter or scene endings: Chapters and scenes typically end with something unresolved or left hanging. If the chapter just stops with nothing to entice readers to read on, the novel doesn't feel like it's going anywhere. Try breaking slow scenes where something is left unresolved, or places where readers will want to know what happens next. Or add a reason for readers to continue with the story in the existing ending.

Not enough scene breaks: A lack of scene breaks can indicate a lot of unnecessary transition description bogging the story down (traveling to get somewhere, filler between scenes that change location). Look for transition summaries between events. Chances are you can cut those and break the scene.

REVISION RED FLAG: If the scenes work at a text level, but the pacing is still slow, or you're getting feedback that the story isn't holding your reader's attention, that could indicate a larger macro problem with the stakes, conflict, or general premise. You might need to go back and examine the core conflict and main goal of the novel. If there's an inherent flaw in the core story, that will affect how the novel reads.

Step Two: Fix a Pace That's Too Fast

Dialogue is fast-paced, as is action, but if you focus too much on those, you'll end up with a breathless ride that goes by too quickly for readers to enjoy.

If There's Too Much Information at Once

A too-fast pace often comes with a lot of action thrown in at the same time, so too much is going on to absorb it all as it goes by. Nothing sticks and readers get confused and stop trying to keep track of it.

To make it manageable, try:

Detangling complicated complications: Having plans go wrong is good, but if every little thing that *can* go wrong *does* go wrong, they all start merging together. Do you need all those problems? Can any be combined or eliminated? Try breaking down the steps of your scenes and see how many tasks the protagonist has to do (and overcome) to reach the end. If the number looks high, or the obstacles are delaying tactics with no consequence (or the same consequence as the other steps), trim a few out.

Adding breathers between action scenes: If the protagonist never gets a chance to catch her breath, readers won't either. Look for places where you can let the protagonist pause and reflect on what's happened to her. These include: right after a problem is discovered, when one is resolved, when she learns something new, when she's stuck and unsure what to do next, etc. Reflection gives you a chance to remind readers why all this matters.

Pruning scenes containing large crowds: A sudden influx of characters (and the names that come with them) can trigger "you can skim over this part" to readers. It's clear they're not supposed to remember all these people, so the scene takes on less importance and flies by. Try naming only those who need to be remembered and limiting the number of people in the scene.

If There's Too Much Action

An all-action plot might be missing the emotional depth that brings its characters to life and fleshes out the world they live in.

Be wary if you see a lot of:

Flat characters: You know those action movies where you can't remember the hero's name? Skimping on characterization is the book equivalent. Give readers time to get to know the characters and care about what happens to them. Offer glimpses into their personalities to slow the pace down when the story is going full tilt for too long.

Blank rooms with no settings: Are you describing the setting enough? Are there enough details for readers to put everything in context? Setting can also be used to raise tension and heighten conflict, and a little goes a long way to slowing a too-fast pace.

Weak motivations: Is the protagonist going through the motions and acting out plot for the sake of plot? If she's just a body "things happen to," the action has no point and becomes background noise. Try showing why you chose this protagonist to handle these problems. Let readers get to know her so they understand *why* she's going through all this trouble. Adding moments of internalization or discussion helps transition scene to scene at a more manageable pace.

If the Text is Too Short and Choppy

Short sentences, short chapters, short scenes. They all pick up the pace, but when used too much, it can be overwhelming.

If everything else seems right, try to:

Smooth choppy sentences: Short sentences are fast. We read them quickly, and the staccato nature adds to the tension of the scene, but there comes a point when it reads like a strobe light, showing freeze-frame images in a row, not a story unfolding. Try mixing it up, using long sentences *and* short quick ones. Use the length of the sentences to adjust the pacing where you need it.

Combine super-short chapters: There is no average size for a chapter, but too many short ones in a row can start to feel disjointed. It's the nature of chapters, since they usually end on that, "Oh no!" moment, but a cliffhanger every few pages never allows for the tension to build. Look at where combining small chapters into one larger chapter would provide a better (and slower) narrative flow. Perhaps turn the small chapters into individual scenes and ease up a little on the dramatic endings for a slower transition.

Add description to talking heads: Dialogue is also fast-paced, but a lot of it without any exposition or stage direction makes it hard for readers to keep up. Check for large sections of dialogue and make sure you have some narrative breaks in there to remind readers who's speaking and provide context for what's happening.

REVISION RED FLAG: If everything is rushing by too fast, that could indicate a weak character arc. The plot side of the novel is working, but there's no character side to provide internal conflict and character growth. Look at how the character arc unfolds and where those more reflective scenes can slow down the story where you need it.

Step Three: Fix a Pace That's Inconsistent

Though more uncommon, sometimes the narrative style contradicts the pace intended, such as having a lot of short sentences and dialogue in a scene you want to unfold slowly.

If the pace doesn't seem right, you might need to:

Map out the pace per scene: Go through the scenes and list the speed of the pacing. If the pace changes in that scene, show that, such as fast > slow (fast, then goes slow). Are there long stretches of one speed? Quick jumps between speeds?

Check the pace against your turning point map: If you have slow-paced scenes during traditionally fast-paced moments (such as key turning points in the plot), try shifting the scenes or changing the pace of those scenes.

Check the sentence and paragraph length vs. the pace desired: Slow-paced scenes typically have longer sentences and more information to absorb. They're also often the more emotional scenes in the novel. Fast-paced scenes use shorter sentences and paragraphs, and contain more action-focused language. If your fast-paced scene has a lot of long and complex sentences, that could be the problem.

REVISION RED FLAG: Sometimes an inconsistent pace results when the novel isn't sure what it wants to be. Check to make sure you're not trying to pace your novel to fit a different type of story or genre from what you wanted to write. For example, if you want a fast-paced thriller, but the novel is paced more like a romantic suspense, you'll want to revise to pick up the pace.

If the general pacing is working, let's take a closer look at how you transition from scene to scene.

If You Want to Smooth the Transitions

Awkward transitions can cause pacing issues, even when your scenes are working well to hold readers in the story. Once readers get into the chapters the text smooths out, but it's a rocky start every time. This can make it tough for readers to start that next chapter, knowing the story is going to drag again before it gets better.

In this session, the goal is to smooth any rough transitions and eliminate jarring areas between scenes and ideas.

Step One: Smooth or Fix Transition Issues

If the pacing is choppy due to rough transitions, identify and revise so the scenes move smoothly from one to the other.

Look for:

Awkward time or location changes: Readers can stumble if the location or time changes without clues to alert them that they've moved. This can also be confusing if the story jumps ahead in time, but it isn't clear how *much* time has passed. Inform readers about a shift, either at the end of one scene or the beginning of another.

Confusing shifts in topics: A shift in ideas that comes out of the blue can also leave readers struggling to catch up. This often happens when the character needs to realize or remember something for plot reasons, but there's nothing in the text to trigger that realization. Try adding that trigger and showing what makes the character suddenly change topics.

Unnecessary travel: Too much time spent showing the transition will cause the pace to drag. Travel is a common problem area for this type, with the character moving from one place to another, often describing everything she sees along the way. In fact, this is sometimes the only reason *for* the travel—an excuse to describe the setting. Break the scene and jump to when the next interesting thing happens.

Scenes that just stop: Be wary of scenes that end with the character going to sleep or stopping, with no sense of something left hanging or where the story might go next. Perhaps end the scene before the action is over, or add a suggestion about what comes next to hand off to the next scene.

Scenes where no decisions are offered: Scenes often end with a character making a decision or choice. No choices means there's nothing to move the scene forward. Try adding a choice or options so the protagonist has several ways to advance the plot.

REVISION RED FLAG: If you have a lot of transition issues, this could indicate a stagnant plot or lack of goals. The scenes focus on individual events, not on a protagonist working to achieve a goal, so the story is a series of, "...and then this happened, then that happened, then this happened."

Step Two: Eliminate Too-Similar Transitions

Since scene beginnings and endings often have similar phrasing, it's not unusual to encounter the same general line repeated throughout the first draft. This can lead to a story that seems predictable and repetitive, even when the scenes *are* different.

For example, be wary if a large percentage of your scenes start with:

- "As I walked into..." and then it describes the room.
- "I stood with..." and then it lists who is in the scene.
- "They waited while..." and then it sets up what's about to happen.

The same opening every time makes readers think they've read the chapter already. The same thing applies to the way you end your scenes and chapters. Look for:

- Characters who go to sleep.
- Declarative "doom and gloom" sentences: "If he didn't find it fast, he was dead."
- Questions about what might come next: "Could they make it to the park in time?"

The same ending can sap the tension from a scene because readers have already seen how that basic ending has turned out. Even if the resolution *is* different, readers might assume they know the answer and thus not wonder or worry about it.

Write down the first and last lines (or paragraphs) of every scene and look for similarities. If you have multiple scenes that start and end in the same way, rewrite to vary. Also, look for repetitive time frames, such as, every time the protagonist has to wait, it's always ten minutes.

Aim for a good mix of transition types, and if possible, try to create a sense of rising tension toward the climax with *only* your opening and ending lines.

REVISION RED FLAG: If most of the scene endings are the same type, that could indicate the scenes themselves are all similar and there's not enough unpredictability in what happens. Make sure every scene has a different fundamental goal, conflict, and stakes so it's not the same scene over and over with different details.

If moving from scene to scene is working well, let's look at how you keep readers turning the individual pages.

If You Want to Strengthen the Hook Lines

Hook lines continuously re-engage your readers and keep your story questions alive. They remind readers what's important, why they like the characters, and what's at stake, so they have reasons to turn every single page of your novel.

In this session, the goal is to strengthen your hook lines to maintain a solid pace for your novel.

There's no set formula for how many hook lines you want per page, so trust your instincts to find the right balance. Put in too many and the manuscript will start to seem like a slew of one-liners. Too few, and there won't be enough to draw readers through the story.

A general rule of thumb: Aim for one to three hook lines on most pages, unless it's an action scene where the high stakes themselves do the hooking. If you don't have at least one hook line per page, that could be a red flag that something is off. You might have too much description or backstory, or your protagonist wasn't driving the scene.

Revision Option: Ways to Develop Hook Lines

Hook lines work well when they're playing on an emotion—joy, sadness, hope, fear, regret, even sarcasm, as that's often covering for strong or repressed feelings. There's a hint of something happening in a good hook line, either a goal stated outright, or a subtle sense of danger or failure.

Develop hook lines in:

Places where you want to emphasize something: A strong hook line can underscore a point for greater impact.

Places you want readers to remember: Good hook lines stand out, so readers tend to remember them.

Places you want to resonate with the theme: Hook lines can summarize and encapsulate an idea or theme that sheds greater meaning on the entire scene—or even the entire story.

Places where you want to create a mood or set a tone: Hook lines can nudge emotions where you want them to go, and help you create the right tone or mood for the situation.

If you're unsure how to craft or develop your hook lines, try to:

Use humor: Make readers laugh and they'll stay with you. Look for places where your protagonist can think or say something funny.

Use emotion: An emotional connection gets readers invested in the story, so bring out points of strong emotion.

Suggest there's more: A hook line combined with a story question is a powerful draw for readers. Can you hint that there's more going on than is being revealed?

Add danger: Hook lines can foreshadow trouble on the way. Can you remind readers of the stakes in a subtle (or not-so-subtle) way?

Get personal: Hook lines usually aren't descriptions. A beautifully written line *can* make readers pause, but it typically will be static, whereas hook lines are active. Personal connections make hook lines *about* something, which draw readers in and pushes them on.

Put them at the ends of the text: Hooks tend to be the last thing readers read, either at the end of a paragraph or all alone on a line. It's the punch right before a pause, so it stands out even more.

🚩 **REVISION RED FLAG:** Don't add a hook line because there's not one on that page. Hook lines work because they fit the scene and highlight some aspect of it that rekindles a reader's interest in the story. A joke for the sake of a joke probably won't work. A joke that fits the scene and says something deeper about it will. Don't force the hooks, *bring out* the hooks.

Hook lines aren't the only way to keep readers on the page though. Sometimes, you need to tease them a little with promises of things to come.

If You Want to Strengthen the Foreshadowing and Reveals

Well-crafted foreshadowing puts readers in the right mindset long before they reach a scene, and makes them anticipate that scene. Secrets unfold in surprising, yet inevitable ways, and readers feel as though the clues were there all along if only they'd seen them—because they *were*.

In this session, the goal is to strengthen your foreshadowing and eliminate any telegraphing that gives the story away.

Step One: Create a Mystery Arc

Do a quick mystery arc to see where critical secrets are revealed, clarify who knows what when, and to determine where the clues are found or hidden in plain sight—you might sneak in a clue but not draw attention to it, knowing it will become relevant later. This will help ensure the protagonist isn't acting on information not yet learned, and allow you to see how your mystery arc unfolds with the rest of the plot.

Look at how the mystery side of your plot unfolds and where readers encounter clues and reveals.

If you're unsure how these elements should unfold, consider:

When and where you want readers to start suspecting the truth: Establishing patterns is a useful foreshadowing technique. Tension builds when readers are expecting something and waiting eagerly for it to happen.

Don't forget the value of the Rule of Three here:

- The first time someone sees something, they merely see it.
- The second time, they notice it, because it stands out now.
- The third time, they're *looking* for it because you've established a pattern to anticipate.

For example, if you want to foreshadow a misunderstanding that has dire consequences, you might have the protagonist misunderstand something minor in the first few chapters. Later on, she might get something else wrong due to distraction. Now you've established a pattern that the protagonist doesn't always listen and misunderstands what she hears. Readers will be looking closely at all her assumptions from then on to see if she's missing something important. When the big moment occurs, tensions will be higher because readers won't know if she's right this time, or if she's missed something yet again.

Or you might drop hints about an item to be used later. When the protagonist arrives at a quaint bed and breakfast for a yoga retreat, she is surprised to see a shotgun hanging above the fireplace and makes a comment. The next guest to arrive notices the gun and makes a joke about it. When the third guest arrives, readers expect the gun will come up again. And that will make them wonder when, where, and how that gun will be used in the story.

Or, you can be more subtle about it and tap into a reader's subconscious. Say you want to foreshadow that blue means bad. You might have the protagonist get into an accident with a blue car early on. Then she has a run in with an office rival who knocks blue ink all over her. You might toss in her snagging her new blue skirt and tearing it right before she goes into an important meeting. After that three-step setup, readers will be *looking* for blue things and anticipating the problems they might cause.

These types of hints can happen over the course of one scene or the whole novel. It's the creak in the night, followed by the thump, followed by the guy in the ski mask jumping out at you.

When and where you want the protagonist to start figuring it out: Readers often spot details long before characters do, but if the clues are *too* obvious, then the characters look dumb if *they* haven't figured them out as well. Check to make sure you have a good balance between reader hints and character hints. If your protagonist needs to know something by page 45, make sure you've left enough clues so the realization feels plausible.

FORESHADOW TIP: *One mystery-writer's trick is to hide important clues in the middle of the paragraph. Readers don't pay as much attention to what's in the middle of a paragraph, but they do focus on the beginning and end of that same paragraph. So they see it, but it often doesn't jump out at them.*

Step Two: Break Any Patterns That Are Too Predictable

Patterns that don't go where we expect them to surprise us. This is the way jokes work: They set up a pattern, then throw in something unexpected as the third item and shock us.

> How do you get to my place? Go down to the corner, turn left, and get lost.

To keep the story unpredictable, lead readers in one direction, then break the established pattern with humor, drama, or even pathos. It works with scenes or a single line. Two scenes set up the pattern, then the third starts off to satisfy that pattern, then—wham!—it changes direction and offers a surprise.

REVISION RED FLAG: Beware of foreshadowing too much. If you're dropping clues every chapter, readers will figure out the secret long before they get to the reveal.

Step Three: Eliminate Telegraphed Details

Telegraphed details can show up anywhere, but here are some common areas to find them:

The deny-it-early conversation: Early in the story, the characters discuss and deny whatever it is that ends up happening later on. It draws attention to the detail you don't want readers to consider, and of course, now that you've mentioned it, they do.

The not-so-random stranger: Someone walks into a scene and gets noticed (often described with more detail than the scene warrants), but is then ignored. At a key moment later in the story, the protagonist remembers this person and it's exactly what's needed to save the day. Or worse—that stranger appears out of the blue when needed.

The obvious pointed-out item: The badge left on the desk, the burning candle, the drip—an item that carries significance is focused on and the protagonist pays a little *too* much attention to it while acting like she's *not* paying attention to it. Readers know this item is going to be important later. In movies and TV shows, this is a slow close up while dramatic music plays.

The overheard news: This *can* be done to great effect, but it can also be a neon sign that something is going to happen. The TV is on as a character walks into the room and the newscaster is talking about something the protagonist will need later. Or the protagonist is out somewhere and encounters two locals arguing about a myth or local legend that will be encountered in a few chapters. The detail *seems* like it's slipped in naturally (it's just background noise after all) but it's obvious instead of seamless because it stands out.

The "little did they know" cliché: Be wary of any phrase that shifts out of the point-of-view character to let readers know something bad is going to happen. For example, "She had no idea what was really in store for her."

Step Four: Add Suggestive and Evocative Details

There have been a slew of movies, TV shows, and Vegas acts that have the protagonist—usually some type of con man—setting up a mark (the victim) to think or respond a certain way. They use subliminal clues to suggest what they want the mark to think or say. Drop enough clues with the numbers three and six in front of someone, then ask them to pick a number between ten and forty, and you'll get a lot of thirty-sixes.

To put ideas in readers' heads, plant a few suggestive clues. Don't explain or draw attention to any of them, but if you want readers to think "blue means bad," then put in something blue whenever something bad happens. Associate blue with bad in their minds, so by the time your protagonist reaches why blue is bad, readers will already feel apprehensive.

Foreshadowing is a handy way to raise tensions, and a well-planned story puzzle leaves lots of clues that readers can look back on and see that the answers were there the whole time.

The final pacing session focuses on your narrative focus, making sure all the work you've done is channeling the story exactly where you want it to go.

If You Want to Tighten the Narrative Focus

Tightening the narrative focus is a time-consuming process that requires going through the entire manuscript and reworking it at the prose level. Not every manuscript will need it, but if all other pacing options haven't cleared up the issues and the manuscript still seems off, it's worth doing.

In this session, the goal is to refocus your narrative to tighten the novel.

To maintain your own focus, try revising one scene or chapter at a time, taking a break between revision sessions. The more focused you are, the easier it will be to focus your narrative.

Step One: Go Scene by Scene and Eliminate Extraneous Details

Look for any off-topic ideas or goals in the text and either cut or revise the text to bring it back on topic. In some cases, you might be able to move the extraneous text to a better scene where it is on topic.

Step Two: Go Paragraph by Paragraph and Refocus the Details

Break up any unfocused paragraphs and regroup them by idea, then add transition sentences to lead readers where you want them to go story-wise. Show what's important and take readers to the next important detail. If you find summarized ideas that feel sluggish or tell-y, you might try dramatizing them instead.

Step Three: Go Sentence by Sentence and Clarify What's Going On

Look for complex sentences where multiple actions are happening at once. "As" is a red flag word here, for example:

> She shed her raincoat as she walked through the door and into the kitchen, dropping her purse on the table as she picked up the note left by her husband.

So much is going on it's hard to tell what the point of the sentence is. Break convoluted sentences apart so each idea is clear and easy to follow, and relates to the paragraph and scene.

Overall, if a detail bogs down the text or goes off on a tangent, consider getting rid of it, or moving it somewhere else where it flows naturally. Beware of irrelevant details that draw focus away from what's important and cause readers to miss the critical information (unless of course, the point is to hide a clue).

You should now have a solid draft (or close to it) that mirrors the vision you had in your head when you came up with the novel's idea. Some manuscripts will be ready for the final look, and if so, skip ahead to Workshop Five: A Final Look on page 197. Others might have a solid story, but either be too long or too short for the target market or audience. If you need to adjust your word count, continue on with Workshop Four: Word Count Work.

Workshop Four: Word Count Work

The Goal of This Workshop: To determine if you need to adjust the word count of your manuscript.

What We'll Discuss in This Workshop: How to cut words from a too-long manuscript, and how to add words and flesh out a too-short manuscript.

Welcome to Workshop Four: Word Count Work

Word counts provide a framework for your novel and a guide to your chosen genre, but the goal is to tell your story to the best of your ability, however many words that is. If a word isn't pulling its weight, cut it. If it's a star performer, let it shine.

Your novel should grab readers from the start, offer them a story they can't put down, and hold that attention until the end. The trick is to make sure every word you use does exactly that. If you have 75,000 words that don't grab a reader, the book will fail, but if you have 140,000 words that grab a reader and don't let go, the book will succeed. It's the story that matters. A great book is a great book.

That said, a published novel *is* a product, and as a product, certain rules apply. These rules exist, for example, to cover the cost of making the book versus what it can sell for, and a book that will cost twice as much due to size isn't economical to sell. Readers won't pay thirty dollars for a 2,500-page paperback (never mind how they'd even *hold* the thing). With e-books and e-book-only publishers, word counts are changing, but the guidelines still do exist, and if you plan to pursue a traditional publishing path, you do need to consider all facets of that.

No matter which path you take, ultimately, it's not how many words you have, but what those words do, that counts.

Analyze the Size of the Novel

When determining the right size for a novel, consider the general ranges of your chosen genre. They will guide you to what readers—and publishers—expect. You want every word used to help the story. It's not about reaching a certain limit, it's about writing the best story you can.

In this session, the goal is to see if your word count is within your target market range and personal goal, and adjust if need be.

A word about word counts: Some writers will be revising a novel with a particular genre, market, or publishing path in mind and need to be within a certain range to sell or publish it. For example, category romances have specific rules that must be adhered to for a particular imprint. If you're not one of those writers, you're not as constrained by word count.

Determine if Your Word Count is Working

Word counts for a typical novel run between 80,000 and 100,000 words. If your novel falls in that range, chances are you're fine for most adult fiction genres and markets. Children's fiction runs 30,000 to 50,000 for middle grade, and 50,000 to 80,000 for young adult. Chapter books run 5,000 to 25,000 words. Picture books come in at under 500. Mysteries often go as low as 60,000 and historical fiction and epic fantasy rise as high as 140,000.

These are *very* general ranges, but if the average size of the genre and market you're aiming for is 60,000 words, your 120,000-word novel is too long. That's like trying to pitch a movie for a 60-second commercial slot.

Be wary of the word-count trap. For every person who says, "You'll never get published with a 145,000-word novel," another will say, "But Best-sellerBob's book was 145,000 words." It does happen, but it's important to remember that those novels succeeded *in spite of the word count,* not because of it. You stand a much better chance at success if you fall within the norms, but if the novel absolutely without a doubt must be that size, then, let it be that size. Just understand that it could be an issue down the road if you plan to publish.

Your chosen publishing path—traditional or self—also affects what's an acceptable word count for your novel. For example, if your goal is a traditional publisher, staying within the standard ranges gives you the best chance at selling your novel. If you plan to submit to an e-book-only publisher or self-publish, word counts can fall outside the norm. No paper means no printing costs and no bulky books, so additional pages aren't as problematic.

Problems Found?

If you find you want to cut back on your word count, spend some time doing the exercises in If You Want to Cut Words From the Manuscript on page 189. If you find you want to increase your word count, spend some time doing the exercises in If You Want to Add Words to the Manuscript on page 193.

If You Want to Cut Words From the Manuscript

Cutting words from your manuscript doesn't have to be a huge hack and slash deal. You don't have to rip your baby to shreds. In fact, hacking away whole scenes often hurts more than helps, because you're killing the story, not the extra words. You want to get rid of the words that *aren't* helping the story.

In this session, the goal is to trim down your manuscript to your target word count range without losing any of your story.

Cutting Words Isn't so Hard. No, Really.

Cutting thousands of words from your manuscript seems daunting, and cutting *tens of thousands* of words can make you want to curl up in a ball and cry, but it's much easier than you think.

Let's look at what "cutting words" really means:

A common "too-long" manuscript is 120,000-words, roughly 480 pages (based on the traditional 250 words-per-page format). You can cut 4,800 words if you delete ten words per page. Ten words is nothing—it's one sentence in most cases, and even in polished and published novels you can still find one sentence per page that can go and not lose any important information. Cut twenty words per page and that's almost 10,000 words gone with little effort. A 150,000-word novel? 600 pages, and 6,000 or 12,000 words gone. Cut thirty words—18,000 words down.

Approaching your edit on a words-per-page basis is much more manageable and allows you to trim consistently across the entire novel, not just certain sections of it.

Step One: Decide How Much You Want to Cut

You might have a fixed number in mind, such as 90,000 words, or a range, such as 80,000-90,000 words. You might also decide to cut in stages, taking out half of the target and then seeing how the manuscript flows before doing anything else.

Step Two: Decide Where it Needs Cutting

Most manuscripts can be trimmed overall, but some will be heavy in one area and need specific trimming. Looking at the novel's structure is an easy way to determine where the extra words are coming from.

Using the basic Three-Act Structure, list the word count of each act (or use whatever structure you prefer and adjust your percentages to fit your structure). Act One is the first 25 percent of the manuscript. The second 25 percent fills the ramp up in act two to the midpoint. The third 25 percent is the ramp down in Act Two from the midpoint. The final 25 percent is in Act Three. So, if your manuscript is 100,000 words, you'd have four chunks of 25,000 words each. At the end of each act, you'd have a major plot turning point.

Remember—these guidelines aren't exact, but if (using the above example) you discover the first act is 35,000 words, but the rest fits the target size for your novel, there's a good chance the beginning is too long and your extra words should be cut from there.

A 10 percent variance in size is fairly normal, but anything beyond that bears a closer look. If you decide an act is working even though it's longer, that's okay. The goal is to use structure to diagnose and identify potential trouble areas, not force your manuscript to fit a particular template.

Step Three: Cut Down the Manuscript

Now comes the tough part, but you can do it. Take it step by step, page by page, and be ruthless. If your instincts tell you what needs to go first, trust them.

Common Areas for Extra Words

Extra words can be found anywhere, but there are a few places where writers tend to babble. Check these areas first when trimming words.

Stage direction in dialogue tags: If the speaker is clear, getting rid of the "she said" tag can help eliminate hundreds of words.

Repeated ideas or thoughts: It's not uncommon to say the same thing in different ways in a scene. Look for multiple details in descriptions, emotional internalizations, and introductions of pretty much anything—these are frequently areas to pile on extra information.

Unnecessary or redundant words: For example, is someone sitting down on the floor? If so, down can go—unless something weird is going on with gravity, sitting on the floor *always* means down. Check your prepositions as well, as most of those can go.

Extra description: A few implied words are often enough to give readers the idea of what something looks like. Let them fill in the blanks so you can save the words.

Characters questioning themselves: Often narrators and protagonists will ask what they should do or wonder about something. It usually reads a lot like them talking to themselves. More times than not, you can trim out these phrases or combine them so they use fewer words.

Overwriting: Look for places where one word can replace several, such as "we went around back to the rear of the store" vs. "We went behind the store."

Tightening the overall writing eliminates the extra words without changing anything.

Revision Option: Tricks to Make Cutting Words Easier

If your words-to-cut number is daunting, it might help to trick your brain into thinking it's not as bad as it looks.

Do the easy cuts first: Empty words, empty dialogue, unnecessary tags—cut all the words that commonly bloat a novel first. You might be surprised at how many "only" "just" and "of the" a novel has.

Cut back to front: If you're cutting words-per-page, start on the last page and work your way toward the beginning. Not only will this keep you from getting caught up in the story, it also won't adjust the page and cause you to cut more words from the front than the back as the novel tightens and becomes shorter.

Cut one chapter at a time in a new file: Copy the chapter into a new file before you trim. It's a lot easier to hit that goal when you can see those words dripping off. And a bonus: By isolating the chapter, you can look at it more objectively and judge the pacing and flow.

Cut one act at a time in a new file: Same principle, with more pages. This can help ensure the cuts are applied evenly throughout the novel.

Set time limits on your cutting sessions: The longer you edit, the more likely it is you'll let something slide because you're tired and want to move on to the next part. Take a break between editing sessions and avoid this temptation.

It's not unusual to need several editing passes to cut down a manuscript. The easiest words tend to go first. Then, if you still need to trim, you have to make harder and harder decisions.

If you need to add words, move on to the next session.

If You Want to Add Words to the Manuscript

We spend a lot of time talking about what to cut from our manuscripts, but there are times when we do need to add words. Maybe you have a novella you want to make larger, or a NaNo (National Novel Writing Month) novel that needs fleshing out, or you fell short of your genre's target range. Even if a novel is the right size for the intended market and genre, you might think the story needs deepening to make it stronger.

In this session, the goal is to find the best way to add words to your manuscript without hurting the story or bloating the narrative.

Step One: Diagnose What's Missing

Before you add anything, determine if you have a sparse manuscript that needs some fleshing out, or a novel that's short on plot. A sparse novel may not need any macro work, while a short-on-plot novel will need some larger additions. Your editorial map will help here, as will your draft analysis from Workshop One.

Plot Check: Look at your plot. Is it too easy to go from inciting event to resolution? Did you skip any steps? If you haven't, do any events need a step or two more to accomplish?

Look for places where if the protagonist didn't win, or outcomes didn't go in her favor, you could tack on a scene or two and add more conflict. Be cautious here though, because you don't want scenes that *take* longer, there needs to be real conflict.

Also look for places where the stakes will go up if the protagonist fails instead of succeeds. Or places where you can raise the stakes if she fails. You want to maintain that sense of problems getting worse and worse or you'll end up with a lot of empty "stuff" happening that doesn't move the story forward.

Subplot Check: Take a peek at your subplots. Are there any points on your main plot line that can be complicated or hindered by braiding in an existing subplot? Can you deepen any of them to give something else in the novel greater meaning? Can they affect the stakes? Do you *have* any subplots? The amount of subplots varies by genre and book, but on average, you usually see one or two subplots in a novel.

Tangent Check: Were there any scenes with goals or ideas you started to explore but decided against it? Those might be subplot ideas your subconscious thought would be fun to develop but didn't, which could be exactly the subplot you need.

Conflict Check: Look for spots where decisions are made. Are the choices too easy? How can you make them harder? And not just physically harder, but emotionally tougher as well.

Clarity Check: Is everything clear? Is the stage direction solid and can readers follow what's happening in every scene? Are the dialogue tags clear so there's no confusion over who's speaking? Is there enough backstory to inform readers about the significance of events? Often these elements get left out because you're terrified of having too much.

World Building Check: This is true for real worlds as well as crafted worlds. Have you done enough with your setting so the world feels real? Real-world writers—have you used enough specific details to make your setting come alive? It's easy to say "New York" and let readers fill in the blanks, but you could end up with flat and lifeless worlds that way. And if your world is created, then you might find some confused readers who feel ungrounded, especially if you used a lot of made-up words.

Internalization Check: Are you in your point-of-view character's head enough? You know why your characters act as they do, but are you getting that all on the page? Pretend you know nothing about them or their history. Are the details readers need to know clear? Short novels often have lots of action, but the emotional aspect is missing—and vice versa.

Action Check: Are you in your point-of-view character's head *too* much? Are you telling or summarizing what's happening and not letting it unfold? Strange as it sounds, action scenes can be boring to write, so it's easy to scrimp on them to get to the more interesting emotional scenes. But it's the balance between head and heart that make the story work.

Backstory Check: Is there an element of the backstory that might be dramatized or illustrated to shed new or better light on something already in the novel? You don't need to add a flashback (unless you do), but a memory of something might cause a different action or response somewhere and take the story to a new place, or even offer a new obstacle to overcome.

Step Two: Flesh Out Where Needed

Once you've identified what's missing, return to the specific workshops and redo the exercises until your manuscript is the right size for the story you want to tell.

The key thing to remember when you're bulking up a novel is to be true to the story. Look for ways to tell that story, deepen those characters, and keep readers guessing what will happen next.

All that's left now is to take one, final look at your manuscript.

Workshop Five: A Final Look

The Goal of This Workshop: To do a final review to catch any issues not previously caught and fixed.

What We'll Discuss in This Workshop: How to know if you're done revising, and how to review your manuscript like a reader.

Welcome to Workshop Five: A Final Look

By the time you get to the final look, you probably want it over. You're sick of the novel, you're tired, and you want to move on to the next step (this is normal, so don't worry). It's a dangerous time, because the urge to send the manuscript out—either to agents, editors, or publishing it ourselves—is high.

Resist the urge.

This is when those "I can't believe I didn't catch that" mistakes happen. You stop seeing what's on the page and see what you want or expect to see. You ignore any nagging thoughts that you *should* fix that subplot, or third chapter ending, or too-similar names, and tell yourself no one will notice.

And someone always does.

Take a break from revising if you need to (a good idea, as it lets you forget what you wanted to do and see what's there), then come back and look at that finished draft and decide if it truly is finished.

Are the Revisions Done?

How do you *know* when a novel is done? When *do* you stop revising? Ultimately that's up to the writer, but you usually have a sense of when you're making novel-changing edits and when you're delaying the inevitable. Declaring a novel "finished" carries a lot of weight and even expectations, so it can be as scary as it is exhilarating. Sometimes, you'd rather keep fiddling with it than send it out.

In this session, the goal is to determine if you are indeed finished with your revision. If you know you're done, skip this session and move onto the final read through.

The easiest way to tell if you're done is to look at the type of changes you're still making.

If You're Making Minor Changes

If all you're doing is tweaking a word here and a comma there—style changes not substance—you're probably done. However, one or two tweaks per page suggests one last proof-reading pass will benefit you. One or two tweaks per chapter suggests it's probably good to go. One caveat here: If the tweaks are errors, keep proofing until you get them all.

If You're Making Story Changes

If you're still tweaking the story, the revisions are not done. In fact, if the story is changing significantly at this stage, that's a red flag that the novel itself isn't finished. You might need to nail down the story and fix it before you can return to the revision.

If You're Making Text Changes

If you're still getting the text right, revising sentences, or moving text around, the revisions *could* be done. If the tweaking isn't changing the story or scenes any, you can skip ahead and polish the text—approach it as a proofreader or copy editor. If the tweaks change the meaning of the sentences and scenes, then you're still revising.

If You're Making Word Count Changes

If you still need to adjust the word count (up or down), the revisions are not done.

If You're Making "Scared it's Not Good Enough" Changes

If you're tweaking out of fear, you're probably done revising. This is a normal fear, and self-doubt about a new project happens to pretty much everyone.

If You're Making "It's Not Quite Right" Changes

If everything *feels* like it's done, but there's something that still bugs you, it could go either way.

On one hand, being tired of the manuscript can easily make you think that it's done when it isn't.

On the other, a finished manuscript you've read dozens of times can seem boring because you've read it so many times.

If the *story* is boring you, that could indicate the story is, well, *boring*. Be objective and determine if this feeling is due to those countless re-reads, or if that scene has always felt blah. Be especially wary of scenes you tended to skip over during revisions because you felt they were "good enough" and didn't want to deal with them anymore. If you were skimming to get through it, you might want to reconsider that scene. Ask yourself:

What about the work feels wrong? If you can pinpoint specific problems, then you're not finished, even if the text is polished to perfection. The issue is likely a macro problem that has nothing to do with the quality of the prose, but a structural or story issue, such as, the pacing is slow in chapter nine, or the goal isn't clear in chapter six, maybe the front half is too long or the stakes are too low overall.

Has that scene or aspect ever bothered you before? Some scenes you know aren't right, but you ignore the warning signs. Often it's because you like the scene and want to keep it, even though you know deep down it should go. Listen to those nagging suspicions that you "ought to do something." Ignore that whisper that says, "No one will notice," or, "I can get away with it." That's a red flag you should fix it.

Uncertainty about a manuscript's readiness is normal, so don't fret if you have doubts. But also know you *can* cross the line between improving your manuscript and editing the life out of it. Stop before you change the text or story *just* so it sounds new.

Review it Like a Reader

Before you declare the novel finished, it's wise to let it sit for a few weeks and then read it straight through, same as if you'd bought it off the shelf. You're not a writer during this read; you're a reader, dying to find your next favorite author and a book you can't stop talking about.

In this session, the goal is to treat your novel the same as the toughest critics you'll ever have—your readers.

Go to wherever you most enjoy reading, using whatever device you prefer—hard copy or e-reader. Review your manuscript as if you were a reader who paid full hardcover price for this book (which means be tough—you deserve a great book for your money!).

When through, answer these questions as honestly as possible:

- ▶ Did the first line intrigue me?
- ▶ Did the first paragraph hook me?
- ▶ Did the first page make me want to read more?
- ▶ Did the first scene grab me?
- ▶ Was there a mystery or story question I wanted to see answered?
- ▶ Was there a suggestion or anticipation that something was about to go wrong?
- ▶ Did every scene make me want to read the next scene?
- ▶ Was there a reason to keep reading on every page?
- ▶ Did the chapters feel like they were going somewhere?
- ▶ Did the middle connect the opening goal and/or the core conflict goal?

- ▶ Did the stakes keep escalating and drawing me through the story?
- ▶ Were the mysteries and story questions interesting?
- ▶ Was I consistently learning new details about the story, world, plot, or characters?
- ▶ Was the voice consistent and enjoyable throughout?
- ▶ Were the characters consistent throughout?
- ▶ Was the final battle worth waiting for?
- ▶ Was the resolution satisfying?
- ▶ Would I tell my friends about this book (be honest)?

If you answered no to any of these, that's a red flag you still need a little more work in that particular area. Return to that session and re-do those exercises.

To check the general pacing and flow of the novel, answer the following questions:

- ▶ Did my mind ever start to wander?
- ▶ Did I notice any unnecessary scenes?
- ▶ Did I skim any scenes?
- ▶ Was I in a hurry to get through any scenes?
- ▶ Did I stumble over any of the text?

If you answered yes to any of these, that's a red flag the manuscript could still use some trimming or editing. Re-examine those scenes and determine what needs fixing.

If you *really* want to dig in for a final analysis, look objectively at the individual story pieces more than the novel as a whole.

Look at the Characters:

- ▶ Did I like the point-of-view character(s) and find them interesting and/or compelling?
- ▶ Did the characters and their actions seem real?

▶ Did the characters feel balanced in their views, attitudes, and opinions (or were they mouthpieces or yes men for the protagonist)?

▶ Did the characters behave in a credible fashion?

Look at the Plot:

▶ Did the plot make sense?

▶ Were the characters' goals clear?

▶ Did those goals advance the story?

▶ Were the goals believable?

▶ Were the stakes high or compelling enough to keep me interested and worried?

▶ Did the stakes seem genuine (not manufactured for the sake of drama)?

▶ Did the overall structure hold together?

▶ Was the plot predictable or did it surprise me (did it read as a fresh story or the same as other novels in its genre)?

Look at the Point of View:

▶ Did the narrative style fit the genre and book style?

▶ Did I feel connected to the point-of-view character(s)?

▶ Were there any points of view that felt unnecessary?

Look at the Description and Setting:

▶ Was I ever bored by too much backstory, exposition, or description?

▶ Did the world feel real and fleshed out?

▶ Was I ever uncertain about what something looked like?

Look at the Dialogue:

▶ Were the dialogue tags clear?

▶ Were the character voices different?

▶ Were there any talking heads in white rooms?

Look at the Pacing:

▶ Was the pacing good?

▶ Was I engaged in the story?

▶ Did I need a break at any time in the story?

If you find anything you'd like to tweak or fix, make those changes now. If everything checks out, declare your revision done!

It's Over!

Congratulations! You made it.

Even revising one aspect of a novel is a ton of work, but the results are usually worth it. Your plot should feel strong and well developed, keeping readers hooked from page one to the end. If this was the only aspect of your novel that needed revision, good luck with the next step, whatever that may be for you.

But first, take some time to celebrate your victory. Revising a novel can be harder than writing it in the first place, and it's an accomplishment that should be rewarded. Go ahead, you earned it.

I hope you've enjoyed the workshops and that they helped turn your manuscript into a solid finished draft. If you've found this book helpful, please share with friends or leave reviews on your favorite sites.

Most of all, best of luck and good writing!

Janice Hardy
December 2017

Appendix

Quick-check analysis questions for easy manuscript review.

Common Red Flag Words

▶ Common self-aware red flag words: She knew, she realized, she felt, she thought. Not every instance will be a problem, but it's a good place to start the search.

▶ Common stimulus/response red flag words: when, as, before. Revise as needed so the stimulus comes first, then the character reaction.

▶ Common telling red flag words: Look for words such as: when, as, to (verb), which, because, to be verbs. These are often found in told prose.

▶ Common stage direction red flag words: Look for words such as, while, when, and as. These often connect multiple actions in one long (and confusing) chain.

▶ Common motivational red flag words: to (action), when, as, while, causing, making, because.

▶ Common emotional red flag words: In (emotion), and with (feeling).

▶ Common descriptive red flag words and phrases: Realize, could see, the sound of, the feel of, the smell of, tried to, trying, in order to, to make.

▶ Common passive red flag words: To be verbs—is, am, are, was, were, be, have, had, has, do, does, did, has been, have been, had been, will be, will have been, being.

▶ Common mental red flag words: realized, thought, wondered, hoped, considered, prayed, etc.

Analyze the Draft

▶ Weak goal-conflict-stakes structures: This could indicate a plot or narrative drive issue.

▶ Lack of character motivation: This could indicate a character arc or credibility issue.

▶ Sparse or missing descriptions: This could indicate a clarity or world-building issue.

▶ Heavy (or missing) backstory: This could indicate a pacing or character issue.

▶ Too many infodumps: This could indicate a pacing or show-don't-tell issue.

▶ Slow or uneven pacing: This could indicate a narrative drive or pacing issue.

▶ Lack of hooks: This could indicate a tension, narrative drive, or premise issue.

▶ Faulty logic: This could indicate a plausibility or plotting issue.

▶ Weak or missing foreshadowing or clues: This could indicate a tension, tone, or description issue.

▶ Areas that need more emotion: This could indicate an internalization issue.

▶ Weak characters and character arcs: This could indicate a character or internal conflict issue.

▶ Weak scene structure: This could indicate a plot or structure issue.

▶ Lack of narrative drive: This could indicate a pacing or goals issue.

▶ Inconsistent point of view: This could indicate a narrative, character, or show-don't-tell issue.

▶ Weak dialogue: This could indicate an infodump, dialogue, or character issue.

▶ Is the point-of-view character(s) likable or interesting enough to read about?

▶ Are their goals clear so there's narrative drive in the story?

▶ Do the characters seem real?

▶ Are there strong and interesting stakes?

▶ Is there too much back story, exposition, or description?

▶ Is the overall structure holding together?

▶ Does the opening scene have something to entice readers to keep reading?

▶ Do the scene and chapter endings entice readers to turn the page?

▶ Is the pacing strong?

▶ Are the plots, stakes, and goals believable?

▶ Does it read well overall?

▶ Do the sentences flow seamlessly or do any stick out and read awkwardly?

▶ Are the dialogue tags clear?

▶ Does the world seem fleshed out?

Analyze the Story Structure

▶ Are all the pieces in the right places?

▶ Does the opening scene present an intriguing problem or mystery to draw readers in?

▶ Is there an inciting event within the first thirty pages (or fifty pages for longer manuscripts) that puts the protagonist on the path to the rest of the novel?

▶ Is there a moment in the beginning where the protagonist makes the choice to pursue the story problem?

▶ Do the stakes escalate at this time?

▶ Does something happen in the middle of the book that changes how the story problem is viewed or approached?

▶ Are the stakes raised again around this time?

▶ Is there a dark moment or setback right before the ending starts that raises the stakes again?

▶ Are the stakes raised yet again?

▶ Does the protagonist make the decision to continue the fight despite the risks or sacrifices?

▶ Is there a clear win for the protagonist at the climax?

▶ Does the ending resolve itself in a way that satisfies the story questions posed in the beginning of the novel?

▶ Is the ending satisfying?

Analyze the Plot and Subplots

▶ Does the plot make sense?

▶ Is there a clear core conflict driving the plot?

▶ Are the characters' actions believable?

▶ Was the plot predictable?

▶ Do events turn out exactly how anyone would expect them to?

▶ Are there enough twists and turns to keep readers guessing?

▶ How often does the protagonist have to make a choice?

▶ Are those choices difficult?

▶ Does the protagonist have approaches different from the other characters' toward solving problems or looking at situations?

▶ Are any leaps in logic or the decision-making process plausible?

▶ Do coincidences work to aid the protagonist instead of hindering her?

▶ Are the protagonist's motivations plausible?

▶ Is someone or something opposing the protagonist?

▶ Does the antagonist have a plan, or does he cause random trouble when the plot needs it?

▶ Is the antagonist trying to win, or does he sometimes act stupidly so the protagonist can win?

▶ Do the choices create conflict between the protagonist's internal and external goals?

▶ Is the protagonist asked or forced to do something that goes against her beliefs?

▶ Are there strong stakes?

▶ Do the stakes escalate as the novel unfolds?

▶ Will the protagonist's life change if she fails to achieve her goal?

▶ Do the stakes affect the protagonist personally?

▶ Is it impossible for the protagonist to walk away from this problem?

▶ Are the stakes clear from the beginning of the novel?

▶ Are the stakes big enough to be worth the reader's time?

▶ What's your goal (as the author) for the subplot?

▶ Are the subplots contributing to the core conflict or character arc?

▶ Will this subplot make the story better, or just longer?

▶ If you took the subplot out, what's lost?

▶ Does it explore a new problem (and likely raise the stakes) or repeat a similar scene or idea you've already done?

▶ Does it require more attention (and words) than the main plot?

▶ Is your protagonist trying to do too much in too many subplots?

▶ Is the subplot compelling enough that readers won't mind the delay in getting back to the main goal, or will they think you're dragging your feet to keep making the problem worse?

Analyze the Scenes

▶ How does this scene serve the story?

▶ How does this scene serve the protagonist's character arc?

▶ How does this scene serve the other characters' arcs? It's not all about the protagonist.

▶ Where does this scene take place?

▶ What is the point-of-view character trying to do?

▶ What goes wrong? What's the problem or challenge?

▶ Why is this important and how does it potentially hurt the point-of-view character?

▶ Who else is in the scene?

▶ What happens right before this scene?

▶ What does the point-of-view character do next?

▶ If you took any scenes out, would the plot change?

Analyze the Narrative Drive

▶ Are the character and story goals clear so there's narrative drive in the story?

▶ Is the protagonist doing something in every scene?

▶ Is there a story point (author's perspective) to every scene?

▶ Is there a story question (reader's perspective) in every scene?

▶ Are these points and questions clear from the start of the scene?

▶ Is the protagonist moving toward something?

▶ Do the scenes and chapters build on one another or are events happening one after another? Does it have a point?

▶ Where is the critical information revealed?

▶ Where do your surprises and twists fall?

▶ Is the protagonist feeling too much?

▶ Is the protagonist debating too much?

Analyze the Tension and Hooks

▶ Is there a sense of something about to happen in every scene?

▶ Are there unanswered questions in every scene?

▶ Is there tension on every page?

▶ Is there tension between characters?

▶ Is there tension in the setting?

▶ Are there moments when the protagonist is relaxed?

▶ Are there big reveals and discoveries throughout the novel?

▶ How many reveals are plot-related?

▶ How many reveals are character-related?

▶ How many reveals are backstory or world-building related?

Analyze the Pacing

▶ What's the common pace for your genre?

▶ Is it well paced overall?

▶ Does it grab you, does it hold your attention, do you want to read on?

▶ Does something change in every scene?

▶ Does the pace speed up during major plot moments?

▶ Are there waves of fast and slow pacing throughout the novel?

▶ Are there any spots that read too fast and readers might have trouble absorbing the information?

▶ Are there any slow spots that might lose readers?

▶ Are there any spots that encourage readers to skim?

▶ Does every scene have an emotional hook?

▶ Does every scene have a mental hook?

Analyze the Transitions

▶ Does each scene end make you want to turn the page?

▶ Is there a sense of anticipation about what will happen next?

▶ Is there a sense of where the plot or story is going?

▶ Does the next chapter's opening scene satisfy reader curiosity, or does it jump ahead in time or location and flash back to deal with the previous chapter's end?

▶ In multiple points-of-view novels, did the next point-of-view character's scene start off with something equally interesting or did the pacing drop and the tension start over?

▶ Does the scene end with something to draw readers forward, or does it let the protagonist sleep, travel, or do something else that drops the tension and pacing?

▶ Does the next scene start with the plot in motion or does it set up the scene to come?

Analyze the Hook Lines

▶ Does every page have an emotional hook line?

▶ Does every page have a mental hook line?

▶ Are there funny or poignant one-liners scattered throughout every scene?

▶ Are there lines that make you smile as a writer on every page?

Analyze the Foreshadowing

▶ Are you foreshadowing the major events or reveals in the story?

▶ Are there any slow or weak scenes that could benefit from adding some foreshadowing?

▶ What emotional scenes might benefit from a little foreshadowing a few scenes earlier?

▶ What "out of the blue shocker information" would seem inevitable with a little foreshadowing to lay the groundwork?

▶ Are there any setup scenes that could do double duty as foreshadowing scenes?

▶ If you had no idea what a clue meant, would it still fit the scene?

▶ Is the clue there specifically to be noticed by readers?

▶ If the reader picked up on this clue and figured it out right then, would it ruin the suspense?

Analyze the Narrative Focus

▶ Is the goal clear?

▶ Does the goal move the scene forward?

▶ Is the bulk of the scene's information supporting this goal?

▶ Does the goal lead to the next scene?

Glossary

Antagonist: The person or thing in the protagonist's path of success.

Backstory: The history and past of a character that affects his or her actions in a novel.

Conflict: Two sides in opposition, either externally or internally.

Core Conflict: The major problem or issue at the center of a novel.

Exposition: Narrative intended solely to convey information to the reader.

Filter Words: The specific words used to create narrative distance in the point-of-view character.

Genre: A category or novel type, such as mystery, fantasy, or romance.

Goal: What a character wants.

Hook: An element that grabs readers and makes them want to read on.

Inciting Event: The moment that triggers the core conflict of the novel and draws the protagonist into the plot.

Market: The demographic traits of the target audience for the novel, such as adult or young adult.

Narrative Distance: The distance between the reader and the point-of-view character.

Narrative Drive: The sense that the plot is moving forward.

Outline: The structured overview of how a novel will unfold, typically written as a guide before the novel is written.

Outliners: Writers who write with a predetermined outline or guide. They know how the book will end and how the plot will unfold before they start writing it.

Pacing: The speed of the novel, or how quickly the story moves.

Pantsers: Writers who write "by the seat of their pants," without outlines. They often don't know how the book will end or what will happen before they start writing it.

Plot: The series of scenes that illustrate a novel. What happens in the novel.

Point of View: The perspective used to tell the story.

Premise: The general description of the story.

Protagonist: The character driving the novel.

Query Letter: A one-page letter used to describe a novel when submitting a manuscript to an agent or editor.

Scene: An individual moment in a novel that dramatizes a goal or situation.

Series: Multiple books using the same characters and/or world.

Set Pieces: The key moments or events in a novel.

Setting: Where the novel takes place.

Sequel (1): A second book that continues where the first book leaves off.

Sequel (2): The period after a scene goal is resolved where the character reflects on events and makes a decision to act.

Stakes: What consequence will befall the protagonist if she fails to get her goal.

Stand-Alone Novel: A novel that contains one complete story in one book.

Structure: The framework a novel is written in, typically based on established turning points at specific moments in the novel.

Tension: The sense of something about to happen that keeps readers reading.

Theme: A recurring idea or concept explored in the novel.

Trilogy: A story that is told over the course of three books.

Trope: An idea or literary device commonly employed in a particular novel type.

Word Count: The number of words contained in a novel.

Thanks!

Thank you for reading Book Two of my Revising Your Novel series, *Fixing Your Plot & Story Structure Problems*. I hope you found it useful!

- Reviews help other readers find books. I appreciate all reviews, whether positive or negative.

- If you enjoyed this book, you might also try the other books in my Revising Your Novel series: *Fixing Your Character & Point-of-View Problems*, and *Fixing Your Setting & Description Problems*.

- Also check out my in-depth Skill Builders series, *Understanding Conflict (And What It Really Means)*, and *Understanding Show, Don't Tell (And Really Getting It)*.

- For planning and developing a novel, try my Foundations of Fiction series, including *Plotting Your Novel: Ideas and Structure* and the *Plotting Your Novel Workbook*.

- I even write fantasy adventures for teens and tweens. My novels include The Healing Wars trilogy: *The Shifter, Blue Fire*, and *Darkfall* from Balzer+Bray/HarperCollins, available in paperback, e-book, and audio book formats.

- **Would you like more writing tips and advice?** Visit my writing site, Fiction University at Fiction-University.com, or follow me on Twitter at @Janice_Hardy.

- **Want to stay updated on future books, workshop, or events?** Subscribe to my newsletter. As a thank you, you'll receive my book, *25 Ways to Strengthen Your Writing Right Now*.

More from Janice Hardy

Award-winning author Janice Hardy (and founder of the popular writing site, Fiction University) takes you inside the writing process to show you how to craft compelling fiction: In her Foundations of Fiction series, she guides you through plotting, developing, and revising a novel. In her Skill Builders series, she uses in-depth analysis and easy-to-understand examples to examine the most common craft questions writers struggle with.

Understanding Show, Don't Tell (And Really Getting It) looks at one of the most frustrating aspects of writing—showing, and not telling. Learn what *show, don't tell* means, how to spot told prose in your writing, and when telling is the *right* thing to do. The book also explores aspects of writing that aren't technically telling, but are connected to told prose and can make prose feel told, such as infodumps, description, and backstory.

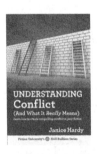

Understanding Conflict (And What It Really Means) looks at how to develop and create conflict in your fiction, and discusses the misconceptions about conflict that confuse and frustrate so many writers. The book also helps you understand what conflict really is, discusses the various aspects of conflict, and reveals why common advice on creating conflict doesn't always work.

Plotting Your Novel: Ideas and Structure shows you how to find and develop stories from that first spark of inspiration to the complete novel. It walks you through how to develop the right characters, find your setting, create your plot, as well as teach you how to identify where your novel fits in the market, and if your idea has what it takes to be a series. Ten self-guided workshops help you craft a solid plot. Each workshop builds upon the other to flesh out your idea as much or as little as you need to start writing, and contains guidance for plotters, pantsers, and everyone in between.

Plotting Your Novel Workbook is the companion guide to *Plotting Your Novel: Ideas and Structure* for those who like a hardcopy approach with easy-to-use worksheets. Its larger workbook format is perfect for writers who enjoy brainstorming on paper and developing their novels in an organized and guided format. No more searching for ideas jotted down on bits of paper. No more losing notes just when you need them most. With more than 100 exercises for the novel-planning process, you can keep all your thoughts in one handy place.

Fixing Your Character & Point-of-View Problems takes you step-by-step through revising character and character-related issues, such as two-dimensional characters, inconsistent points of view, excessive backstory, stale dialogue, didactic internalization, and lack of voice. She'll show you how to analyze your draft, spot any problems or weak areas, and fix those problems. Five self-guided workshops show you how to craft compelling characters, solid points of view, and strong character voices readers will love.

Fixing Your Plot & Story Structure Problems guides you through plot and story structure-related issues, such as wandering plots; a lack of scene structure; no goals, conflicts, or stakes; low tension; no hooks; and slow pacing. She'll show you how to analyze your draft, spot any problems or weak areas, and fix those problems. Five self-guided workshops show you how to craft gripping plots and novels that are impossible to put down.

Fixing Your Setting & Description Problems focuses on setting and description-related issues, such as weak world building, heavy infodumping, told prose, awkward stage direction, inconsistent tone and mood, and overwritten descriptions. She'll show you how to analyze your draft, spot any problems or weak areas, and fix those problems. Five self-guided workshops show you how to craft immersive settings and worlds that draw readers into your story and keep them there.

Acknowledgements

As always, this book would not be here without the help and support of some amazing people.

I couldn't do this without my husband Tom. He's always there with the right words of encouragement—or the right amount of nagging—to keep me going when I need it.

Ann—a gal couldn't ask for a better crit partner. I'd be lost without your sharp eyes and insightful comments. You make me a better writer and I'm honored to call you friend.

And a big hug to all my beta readers on this book: TK Read, Chris Bailey, Lisa Bates, Trisha Slay, Beth Letters, and Dario Ciriello. You guys rock, and I appreciate all the help you gave me.

My Fiction University readers. You guys are the best, and your dedication to your craft, curiosity about the writing process, and your eagerness to learn are a constant source of inspiration for me. Hearing from you always makes my day.

Thank you all.

About the Author

Janice Hardy is the founder of Fiction University, a site dedicated to helping writers improve their craft. She writes both fiction and nonfiction.

Her nonfiction books include the Skill Builders series: *Understanding Show, Don't Tell (And Really Getting It)* and *Understanding Conflict (And What It Really Means)*, and the Foundations of Fiction series: *Plotting Your Novel: Ideas and Structure*, a self-guided workshop for planning or revising a novel; its companion guide, *Plotting Your Novel Workbook*; and the *Revising Your Novel: First Draft to Finished Draft* series.

She's also the author of the teen fantasy trilogy The Healing Wars, including *The Shifter*, *Blue Fire*, and *Darkfall*, from Balzer+Bray/Harper Collins. *The Shifter* was chosen by the Georgia Center for the Book for its 2014 list of "Ten Books All Young Georgians Should Read." It was also shortlisted for the Waterstones Children's Book Prize (2011) and The Truman Award (2011).

Janice lives in Central Florida with her husband, one yard zombie, two cats, and a very nervous freshwater eel.

Visit her author's site at janicehardy.com for more information, or visit fiction-university.com to learn more about writing.

Follow her at @Janice_Hardy for writing links.